I mean that literally, because in my research for this and my other retail books, I researched the best retail stores across the globe.

Most retailers underestimate the relevance of store design and visual merchandise display to their success.

Your selling environment determines: The customers you attract and the price you can charge.

The retail business is 'showbiz', the extent to which you are willing to put up a great performance for your customers is the extent to which you are going to succeed.

The goal of this book is to teach you the psychology and strategies of designing a beautiful store.

Harrods success is based upon three things:

- Good store design
- Beautiful visual merchandise display
- Effective loss prevention strategies

My aim is to teach you how to replicate a Harrods-like store design to enable you sell a made in China toy bus for three times the price it is sold for at other retailers.

This book is not about changing or improving upon what you are already doing: it is about the hidden opportunities in your retail business you have not paid attention to.

It is my guarantee to you that you will easily triple or even quadruple your profit margin in less than 90 days by implementing a third of the information in this book.

During my research for this book, I visited Harrods. I have heard a lot about Harrods, but had not actually visited it. When my sister visited me from the States, Harrods was on her list of places to visit. However, by the time we arrived, it was already closed for the day.

You can imagine my anticipation and apprehension at visiting one of the most famous retail stores where royalties, Hollywood A-list stars and the "who is who" from around the world go shopping.

In my mind, everything in Harrods was made of gold. I even bought a special outfit for the occasion to ensure I was in sync with the royalties and A-list stars.

I was hoping I could catch a glimpse of Roman Abramovich and some of his billionaire friends or some Saudi prince.

However, instead of Russian oligarch or Middle Eastern Sheikh, what caught my attention was a bus.

I had bought the identical bus for my son from ASDA. It was the same bus in the same packaging.

An odd question popped into my mind when I noticed the bus: why is it that the same bus, in the same packaging, probably made in the same factory in China, by the same people, being sold in Harrods for almost three times the price it was sold for in ASDA?

At first it was a mystery to me. But as I walked around Harrods the answer came to me.

ASDA sells toy bus. Harrods sells classy toy bus even if it is made in the same factory in China.

There is a distinction and that distinction is what this book is about.

The price of a product is not determined by the cost of bringing that product to the marketplace as we are taught in business school rather by *who is buying, how much they are willing to pay and how the product is sold.*

The reason the same bus, made in the same factory in China is sold in Harrods for almost three times the price it is sold for in ASDA, comes down to *who shops at Harrods and how the bus is sold to them.*

For a start, cheapskates like me are not Harrods target market. Harrods know their target market is oil Sheikhs and Russian oligarchs whose focus is not on the products but on the manner in which the product is sold to them.

This is a very important point I will like you to take from this book. Most retailers fail because they ignore this simple but fundamental marketing principle. The majority of retailers do not even know their target market.

They open their stores, stock them with goods and hope that customers will show up simply because they are open for business.

This is a very big mistake!

You first need to decide who you want to sell to and then create a selling environment to attract those types of people.

Harrods have obviously decided who they want to sell to, therefore, they created a selling environment that appeals to only those types of people.

Their store design and visual merchandise display are created to appeal to their target customers.

Harrods has one of the best store design and visual merchandise display in the retail industry…period.

About the Author

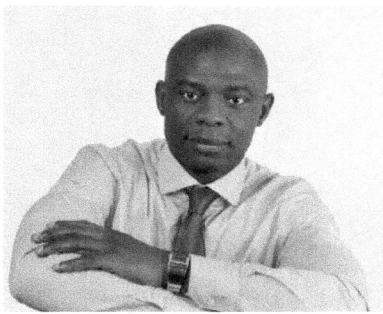

Romeo Richards is the founder of the Business Education Centre, an institute that shows professional entrepreneurs such as doctors, lawyers, dentists, consultants, trainers, coaches, and security firm owners how to make "7 Figure" in twelve months. He is also the creator of the Business Success Quadrangle Framework and The Blue Ocean Strategy Canvas for: doctors, lawyers, dentists, consultants, retailers, coaches, trainers and security firms.

He has authored eight books on retail profit improvement and is currently writing four additional books on retail store design, visual merchandising, how to market a retail store and how to make profit in retail and the "How to effectively market and manage a professional firm" series for doctors, lawyers, dentists, consultants, trainers, coaches and security firms.

He has authored several White Papers and regularly writes articles on entrepreneur development, retail profit improvement and speak on the same.

Store Design Blueprint

How to Design an Attractive but Profitable Store

Romeo Richards

www.theprofitexperts.co.uk
+44(0)78 650 49508
romeo@theprofitexperts.co.uk

© Copyright Protected; 2013. The Business Education Center. All Rights Reserved.

Dedication

I wrote about vision as your reason for doing anything. I do what I do first and foremost to be an example to my son.

Secondly, to have the ability to help my people shed the curse of poverty.

Alex this book is for you!

Africa this book is in your honour!

Table of Contents

About the Book i

About the Author v

Dedication ix

Acknowledgements xiii

Why You Should Read This Book xvii

Introduction xix

Chapter One: The Psychology of A Beautiful Store Design 1

Chapter Two: How To Increase Retail Sales With Attractive Store Design 15

Chapter Three: How to Increase Retail Sales With Brand Image Selling 39

Chapter Four: Designing Store For Increase Customer Flow 49

Chapter Five: How To Choose Your Store Colour And Layout 59

Chapter Six: The Best Retail Store Lighting System 67

Chapter Seven: How To Wow Customers With Creative Storefront Design 79

Chapter Eight: How To Choose The Right Materials For Store Design 89

Chapter Nine: How To Design A Profitably Retail Store 103

Chapter Ten: The Best Store Design Technologies 111

Summary 115

Great Books by Romeo 117

Book Romeo 126

Acknowledgements

My sincere gratitude to Mr. White, John and Michael for editing the book.

Thanks Jen for formatting it and Joseph for managing the entire project.

Store Design Blueprint

How to Design an Attractive but Profitable Store

Romeo Richards

www.theprofitexperts.co.uk

+44(0)78 650 49508

romeo@theprofitexperts.co.uk

Why You Should Read This Book

Why should you read this book when there are literally thousands of retail store design books on the market?

For a start, it is the only book on store design that talks about the only thing you are interested in: profit.

How can you make profit in your retail store?

You make profit by:

- Increasing sales
- Increasing customer satisfaction
- Increasing staff productivity
- Decreasing shrinkage

In this book, we teach you how to achieve the above objectives through the use of beautiful yet secure store design.

No other book on store design has ever connected store design to those four critical success factors and profit.

There are fundamental principles which underpin good store design:

- Customer attraction
- Customer flow
- Persuasion to buy
- Shrinkage management

Your ability to effectively embed these elements into your store design strategy will determine your level of success. This book outlines the process for embedding those four elements into your store design and sales strategy.

It outlines the best store design strategies used by the most successful retailers in the world…Strategies when effectively applied, will propel you to unbelievable success.

And here is the icing on the cake, your competitors do not even know most of these strategies. So what you have in your hand is the missing piece of the retail success secret…The ultimate store design blueprint secret.

Introduction – Store Design

If you are a horror film junkie you always know when a horror film is about to reach its climax.

If the scene is set in a house, you will notice the camera moving up and down the stairs…then the window flings open…and the moon starts shinning directly into the room…wind begins to blow…the light starts blinking on and off…on and off…and you hear the clock tick…tick…tick…then there is the sound of footsteps in the corridor…then the shadow of the antagonist appears…and then zoom!…without warning the antagonist attacks.

In horror film after horror film, this identical scene plays out all the time. Whether the film is being shot in a house, in the night or day or out in the woods, the costume design and the choreography is always the same.

Why is this always the case with horror and most successful films?

Answer: the directors of horror films understand that the intrigue of the film is not just about the killing or the plot. It is also about the costume design, the sound, the lights, and the background.

When someone goes to watch a horror film, they already know someone is going to die. Therefore the directors understand that the killings no longer scare the audience, it is the events leading to the killing that are intriguing.

What does horror films have to do with retail store design and what lesson can the retail industry learn from horror films?

The lesson the retail industry can learn from horror films is this: it is not about the merchandise; it is the presentation of the merchandise that matters to the customers.

A good store design captures the imagination of its targeted audiences just like a good film does. The store is a theatre where customers come to watch spectacular displays of merchandises. If they like the display they will buy, if they don't like the display, they will leave.

The success of great films stems from their ability to cleverly manipulate people's psychology through the brilliant use of words and costume design.

Retailers can do well to emulate the cleverness of the film industry in the presentation of their merchandise if they intend on achieving similar success.

This books aims to show retailers how to choreograph their store design to achieve similar success.

The first half of the book deals with the psychology of store design. It addresses the questions of understanding your target market and using your brand image to attract customers.

The second half of the book deals with the best materials to use for your store design. I go into the best lighting system, fixtures, wall, flooring, ceiling and technologies.

Your success as a retailer rests on your ability to create the type of shopping environment that will entice customers to visit your store.

The retail environment is changing. These days you are not only competing against other retailers, you are also up against some guy sat in his room selling stuff on the internet.

Consequently, you need to understand that the strategies that worked a few years ago will not work in the new retail environment.

You need a new strategy.

This book contains the new strategies you need to succeed.

Chapter One

The Psychology of A Beautiful Store Design

Harrods is one of the more successful retailers in the world. In 2011, in the thick of the global financial crisis; the London based retailer's annual sales were in the region of a billion pounds. When thousands of well-known retail brands were struggling to survive and some forced to close shop.

What is it that makes Harrods more successful than most retail organisations?

Harrods success can be attributed to the following three factors:

- Good store design
- Attractive visual merchandise displays
- Effective loss prevention strategy

The ability to design their store or create visual merchandise displays that incorporate all these elements is one of the determining factors for the success of Harrods and many of the world's most successful retailers.

Harrods' store design is in a class of its own. It is unique, innovative and clever. One important element of their store design is the concept of the stores inside. The store is designed in such a way that as customers move from one department to the next, they get the feeling of moving from one store to another in a shopping centre. Whoever conceived that design concept provided Harrods with a huge competitive advantage over its competitors.

Harrods's visual merchandise displays are as attractive and inviting as displays can get. As customers move from one designer outlet to another; they are met by a completely different display that is indicative of that designer. It is as if the designers themselves went into Harrods to arrange the displays.

Store design and visual merchandise displays need to serve four objectives:

- Attract potential customers as they pass by the store
- Entice those potential customers to enter into the store
- Maintain their interest whilst they are in the store
- Persuade them to buy.

Harrods' ability to effectively utilise these four principles in its store design and visual merchandise displays has been responsible for its phenomenal success.

In his book "Blink", author Malcolm Gladwell introduced the concept of thinking without thinking. "Blink" "the power of thin slicing" and "rapid cognition" is the type of thinking process that occurs in the blink of an eye.

As shoppers walk through a shopping mall of two three hundred stores or a busy high street, they are thin slicing each and every store.

What entices them to choose one store over the other is what Mr. Gladwell alluded to in his first book "Tipping Point"…the little things that make a huge difference. Some of the little things determine whether someone enters your store as opposed to that of your competitor is your store design.

As one walks around Harrods, it is evident that their success does not stem from 'Made in China' products that can be found in stores all over the UK. Their success comes from their ability to apply the principles from "Blink" and the "Tipping Point" to their store design and visual merchandise displays.

Harrods success can be linked to its belief that little things make a big difference:

> Little things like having store associates within easy reach of every customer
>
> Little things like the extraordinary use of mannequins

Harrods success also results from having one of the best store designs and visual merchandising display in the retail industry.

What is Store Design Psychology?

All retailers strive to satisfy every customer that enters their store and give them the kind of service they desire. Offering good customer service and fine quality products are a given in the retail business. But a core element that attracts customers into a retail store is the aesthetics of the store.

The majority of shoppers are more likely to enter a store and purchase when the store has an attractive layout and is convenient for shopping. The key in persuading more shoppers to visit a store lies in it having an attractive store design.

Every retail store has a unique design which entices shoppers into the store. Retail stores are designed to generate an easy and delightful shopping experience. A very important element in retail store design is the psychology that augments the design.

The large windows endowed with eye-catching designs; aisle widths and rack heights are carefully detailed to create a positive feeling which lures shoppers into a store.

All four corners of the store must be viewed and evaluated accurately. The wall colours, signage, checkout counters, racking schemes, displays, and other areas form part of the store layout.

The interior design of a retail store plays a key role in attracting shopper and increasing sales. Proper placement of props such as mannequins and racks help the store to appear more attractive. Creating a theme also helps develop vibes that entice shoppers.

A well designed store makes it convenient and easy for customers to shop. When a shop creates a design concept that matches with the products they are selling, it makes it easier and appealing for the customers to buy.

Furthermore, having a colour scheme that matches the products adds more pleasure for customers to shop. The right colour scheme creates a positive mood for the customer when shopping. For example, a baby clothing store that uses light pastel colours reflects the target market.

The majority of people derive pleasure from shopping in a light and spacious environment. A spacious and clutter-free store is also an advantage for you and your employees.

It becomes easy for your store associates to watch over products and reduce shoplifting. Tables in the central areas, cabinets and shelves towards the back walls create the illusion of a more spacious store.

Apple stores are always packed as customers just love hanging out in their stores. The Early Learning Centre is a children's toy store in the UK. I have been to a few of them and noticed there is not enough space for children to sample toys. You cannot have a toy store that is compact; you lose the potential for sale.

Some retail store designs tend to be excessive. Excessive and unnecessary use of colour and other design elements results in the opposite effect. Instead of enticing shoppers into the store, it repels them.

Therefore, striking the balance between an attractive store that serves as a magnet for shoppers and one that repels them needs an understanding of store design psychology.

Most retailers forget that retailing is about sales and marketing. The most effective marketing strategy a retailer has at his disposal is a well-designed store and attractive merchandise displays.

When there are two or three hundred stores in a shopping centre, the difference between deciding to enter in or pass by a store rests on the design of the store front.

When customers are in a store there needs to be a reason for them to stay longer. The longer they stay, the higher the chances of them buying.

The three main aspects of a store design that keep customers engaged for longer are:

- Designs that enables good customer flow
- An attractive and good lighting system
- Overall atmosphere of the store

Why do people buy?

Why do people buy? We all buy for diverse reasons. The human thought process is complex and irrational. Even though we try to rationalise our actions based upon artificial environmental factors; the reality is, we all do things for the same three reasons:

- Status
- Survival

- Sex

What does everyone want?

In marketing we are taught to believe that individual's wants are different.

This statement is true to an extent but not exactly true. Human psychology has not changed since the dawn of time. The same desire humans had when we lived in caves; we still hold those desires today.

Every prospect, client or customer wants the following three things:

- Result
- Solution
- Relief from something

How these three things manifest themselves in our brain takes the form of the products and services we choose to buy. However, the fundamental principle is this: in the final analysis when customers take out their credit card to buy a product or service, no matter what that product or service is, they are doing so to satisfy all or at least one of the above.

Being aware of that, as you prepare to design your store, here are some questions that should be going through your mind:

1) Which one of the above three are you marketing to satisfy with your store design?
2) Which one of the three are you marketing to satisfy with your shop window display?
3) What emotion are you aiming to trigger?
4) What result should they imagine your store is going to produce for them?

5) What solution should they think your store design would provide?

6) Finally, what pain is the store design going to relieve?

This is not to say that when someone enters your store they will achieve all of those results, your store design just needs to plant the perception of those results in their minds.

But there is a catch. The store designer needs to know the benefit and hidden benefit. It is only when the store designer knows the benefit behind the benefit that they will be able to create a beautiful and attractive store design that captivates your target market.

Figure 1: Think of the benefit behind the benefit in your display

I will use Victoria's Secret as an example. A woman passing by a Victoria Secret store spots sexy lingerie in the shop window; her first thought is: I will look sexy in that or that bra would prop up my cleavage.

But here is the catch, that bra would prop up her cleavage not because she just wants her cleavage propped up but to attract the opposite sex. (I must add a disclaimer that here I am not trying to be sexist I am just using this as an example.)

Therefore as you design your store, your aim should be to match the thinking of the shopper with your store design. Do not design your store to appeal to the beauty of the breast but the outcome that the beautiful breast will result in – the opposite sex!

A major part of store design is being able to analyse shoppers thought process. As was alluded to previously, the human thought process is complex and irrational. The human brain is set up with areas for various functions.

There are three brain types:

- Retile
- Mammal
- Thinker

The problem is these three brains are not integrated. They work separately. The thinking brain is the least dominant of three, which is why our thinking process is in most cases irrational. In the majority of cases, our decisions are based upon triggers from the unconscious.

Remember "Blink"? The power of "thin slices" and "rapid cognition"; this is our predominant thought pattern.

Thin-slicing is a psychological term for the ability to find patterns in events based upon minimal information. It means making rapid decisions with the least amount of information.

When an individual walks through a mall of three hundred stores or on a High Street on Saturday afternoon; his mind races and he thinks at a fast rate. The decision as to which store he enters is made in a blink of an eye.

The merchandise display and store design that catches his attention will win his patronage. Except if he had pre-planned a visit to a particular store; his decisions are based purely upon thin slicing each store as he walks.

Many of our actions, behaviour and thinking originate from the adaptive unconscious, which the majority of us are unaware of.

However, the good news for the retail industry is…other humans are capable of altering those unconscious biases just by tinkering with the little details.

In "The Tipping Point" as I pointed out earlier, Malcolm Gladwell demonstrated how to tinker or social engineer humans to get them to behave in ways we would like them to.

The retail landscape is changing rapidly. Too many choices; disruptions and hoards of information from all directions, either confuse or overwhelm customers.

As the customer walks through a shopping mall, there are gazillion things going through his head. Yours is not the only store in the shopping mall neither is it the only stores design he had seen on that day.

Figure 2: Your window display has to be attractive enough to capture shoppers as they walk pass your shop

There is a cluster of information and stores all around him. Therefore, in order to ensure that your store stands tall above the rest, you need to design it to match his thinking process. That can only be done when you understand store design psychology and use it as a framework for designing your store.

People don't like to be sold but they love to buy, so your store design should sell to them without peddling to them.

The most effective store designs are those that speak directly to the customer's desire for:

- Result
- Solution
- Relief from something

Remember! It is all about:

- Status
- Survival
- Sex

To achieve the above effectively requires you do the following:

- Identify your target market
- Find out what appeals to them
- Incorporate it into your store design

How to apply the principle of store design psychology?

To influence shoppers buying behaviour and design a store that appeals to them demands an in-depth research into your target market's buying habits. This can be done in-house or through an external research agency.

The following steps would assist you implement the psychology of store design effectively:

Step 1:
Conduct, or hire an outside research firm to research into your target market. Using the aims and objectives of your business as a guide…the age, gender, or income group you intend to serve.

Step 2:

Create a store design blueprint tailored to your target market. Focus on colours; types of material; flooring; lighting and fixture arrangement.

Step 3:

Focus the store design on customer flow. This means the aisle width, height and size as well as the location of check-out counters.

Step 4:

Incorporate security and loss prevention into the store design. Pay attention to the location of your entrance and exit, staff areas and warehouse.

A good store design leads to: increased sales, improved staff productivity, reduced shrinkages and increased profit. However, this cannot be done without taking into consideration the psychology of the process.

Things to consider in your store design blueprint:

Display fixtures:

Figure 3: Ensure you consider the types of fixtures you will eventually use when designing your store

Display fixtures are essential components of a retail store design. Consequently, it is essential they are added to the original blueprint.

Lighting system:

Figure 4: Good lighting system enhances the appearance of your store

Lighting plays a crucial role in a retail environment. Lighting has to be a part of the store design blueprint. There needs to be adequate lighting to enhance product appearance.

The placement of the lights should be considered as lights need to be adjusted to accommodate the store layout and climatic conditions.

Fittings:

Figure 5: Fittings need to complement not confuse shoppers

Fittings such as hanging chandelier in the middle of the store, large clock at the rear of the counter and other designs that complement the store's overall appearance need to be also taken into consideration.

Fittings need to be kept to a minimum to avoid confusing the customer. The objective of a store design is to enhance merchandise, not to be points of focus.

Maintaining the ideal design of your store would result in increased sales and brand awareness. Always ensure that you create a lighter aura and a clutter-free store design.

Chapter Two

How To Increase Retail Sales With Attractive Store Design

I have received internet marketing training from the best internet marketers in the world. These are guys who together make billions on the internet each year. Therefore, when attending their training, one would expect them to teach techniques and tricks for making money on the internet.

But whether their training is for a day or a weekend, they spend very little time teaching techniques for using the internet effectively. Instead they focus exclusively on marketing fundamentals. I remember asking one of them during a training section why is it that they do not teach techniques for using the internet effectively. He responded that participants will not be able to effectively use the internet to market their products or services if they do not know basic marketing fundamentals.

Come to think of what he said as I write this book, I believe he was absolutely right. The most successful businesses are not successful because of the industry they are in or because of the product or services they provide; they are successful because they apply simple business and marketing fundamentals.

Apple is a typical example of a business that is not successful because it sells the best products in the world. Its success is based upon the fact that its products function.

Apple's product design is based on three principles:

- Functionality

- Simplicity
- Elegance

Prior to the release of a new Apple product there is the usual hype and buzz around about how good the product is going to be. However, when the product is released the recurrent question that always pops up is what was all the fuss about? There is nothing extraordinary about the product design yet it outsells its competitors. So the question that comes to mind is why is Apple able to outsell its competitors all the time?

Answer: Apple products are functional.

When Apple is about to release a product, its focus is not on how cool the product is going to look but how would it make the life of users easier or even how could it change their lives.

Apple designers go into the head of the average buyer of an Apple product and ask the questions:

Who is the person we are producing this product for?
What work does he do?
Where does he live?
How would this product make his work or home life easy?
What else would he be able to do with this product?
How can this product change his life for the better?

It is only when Apple designers are able to provide answers to the above questions would they embark on the process of designing the product.

Similar thought process goes into the design of cars, whether it is Mercedes-Benz, BMW or Ferrari, their designers ask themselves those question prior to designing their cars.

Mercedes-Benz appeals to a completely different market from BMW or Ferrari. While the average Mercedes-Benz owner might be focused on comfort or luxury, the BMW or Ferrari owner might be focused on speed. Therefore as the designers of these automobile manufacturers sit to design their cars, they concentrate on fulfilling the desires of their target market.

Google arguably one of the most successful businesses of our time has the same web page that it had when it started. Even though it 'Googelise' its logo every day, the design of the webpage remains the same. Which is one of the main reasons it over took other search engines and it continues to dominate the search engine market.

What does the information regarding Apple, Google and automobile manufacturers have to do with retail store design?

Everything!

Retail store design like any other design is subject to similar design principles. In order for a retail store to achieve similar phenomenal success as any other successful business, retail stores have to conform to the same fundamental business principles that make other businesses successful.

For most of this book I am going to use Harrods as an example of a good retail model. The reason for this is that Harrods is one of the most successful retailers in the world.

Therefore, there is no better example to use than one of the most successful retailers in the retail industry. As I searched for the secret behind Harrods' success, I came to the conclusion that the key is its application of the five fundamental business principles:

- Visionary leadership
- Great people

- Good system
- Good marketing system
- Good business model

Take its marketing strategy in its children section for example. When you enter Harrods children, you will first notice play consultants playing with the toys and asking parents and their children to join in the game.

This is basically moving further from just having the children seeing and touching the toys to actually having to play with them to get them emotionally invested in the toys.

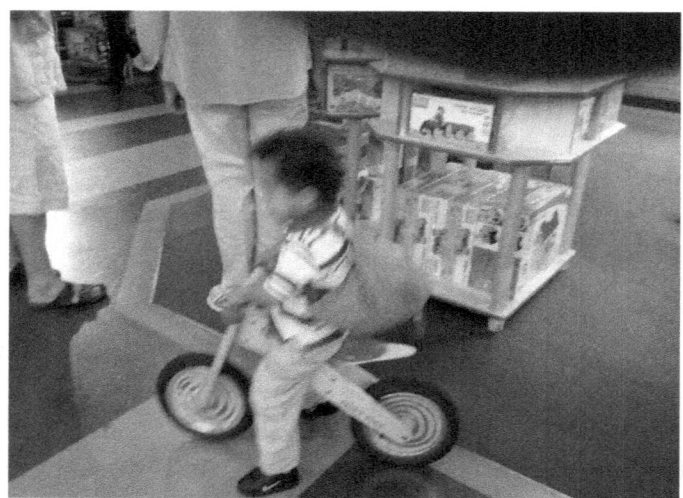

Figure 6: Harrods creates the atmosphere for children to sample their toys

After playing with the toy, how many kids will not automatically want to take the toy home with them to continue playing.

In contrast to Harrods, when children and parents enter the Early Learning Centre, it is like a dental suite. The stores is crammed one can hardly breathe. There is nowhere for the children to sample the toys.

Figure 7: Early learning centre stores are like soviet dental suite

Do you see the difference?

Do you see now why it is critical to learn marketing fundamentals before you consider designing your retail store?

One thing you need to learn from the onset is this: the fundamentals of business never change. They remain the same whether it is for the HSBC bank in the city of London or a cleaning business in a dusty New Delhi ghetto. The fundamentals of business are similar to the fundamentals of science or engineering.

The formulas that were used in chemistry since the times of the Roman Empire or the civilization of Egyptian apply to today's chemistry. There might be slight modifications and advancements but the fundamentals remain the same.

The same applies to business. Every successful business has the same five components that make it successful:

- Visionary leadership
- Great people
- Good system

- Good marketing system
- Good business model

The absence of any of the above will cause any business to fail. These are core principles. They are not just something that might be good for a business, they are elements that businesses cannot survive without.

The aim of this chapter is to outline the process of increasing retail sales with attractive store design using those five business success fundaments.

In a book on store design, you will expect techniques and strategies on ways of designing your store to increase sale. However, the best strategies will not work if the person implementing the strategy does not know the reason they are implementing them.

This chapter and the next one would specifically answer the question: why it is important for a retail stores to be designed in a specific way.

I am of the belief that it is only after you have grasped this concept would you be able to derive the maximum benefit from the technique and strategy I will be outlining in subsequent chapters.

However, my aim in this book is not to address the five business fundamentals, I will be dealing with the forth component: a good marketing system. It is my belief that marketing is the most essential of the five business fundamentals.

Conventional wisdom holds that a business cannot make a profit until its third year of operation and we have all bought into that lie. I am here to tell you that, this belief is completely false.

A retail store can begin to make profit from its first month of operation if it applied the principles written in this book. The application of those five core elements is a insurance against any retail business failure.

Understanding how to increase retail sales is very crucial for the success of any retail business and more so now with the increasing failure of many retail businesses.

Background

Lingerie specialist La Senza went into administration in the first week of 2012. It is amongst some 183 UK retailers including: Barratts, Clinton Cards, Habitat, HMV, Focus DIY, JJB Sports, Jane Norman, Mothercare, Oddbins, TJ Hughes and Thorntons that got into trouble in 2011. This is in addition to the thousands of retailers that went bust without making the headlines.

The British Prime Minister alarmed by the prospects of many UK town centres turning into ghost towns, appointed a committee headed by UK retail guru, Mary Portas, to look into why the UK High Street was at risk of extinction.

Her report concluded that the main reason for the demise of the High Street was:

"High Streets have reached 'crisis point' with the rise of super-malls, out-of-town supermarkets and internet shopping".

This follows another report by Colliers CRE which highlighted the "downward spiral and degenerating or failing" of the UK High Street.

As I write this book, the Australian government has also commissioned a report into the future of the Australian retail industry.

So why is the retail industry facing such difficulty even though literally no one can survive without visiting a retail store?

The answer to this question is simple:

The retail industry is the only industry where increased sales area is the key performance indicator.

A large part of this chapter was written as a White Paper on Boxing Day (2011), which is the day when most retailers start their biggest sales of the year. The irony is even though they make their biggest sales on that day, the large majority of retail stores did not make a single red penny in profit.

How can a business expect to make a profit from discounting products at 50% or 70%? Retail profit is an average of 3%. Even the most profitable retailers make between 3 and 5% profit.

The large majority of retailers make a profit margin of between 1.5–3%. Therefore, if a retailer is making a 3% profit margin and is discounting his merchandise by 50%, how much profit will he be making?

I am aware that it might sound contradictory that I am writing a chapter on how to increase retail sales with attractive store design yet seem to be criticising the concept of increasing sales.

I would like to clarify the fact that I am not critical of the concept of increasing sales, increased sales must also simultaneously result in increased profit.

> *To increase sales without simultaneously increasing profit is a wasted opportunity.*

Therefore, my aim in this chapter is to show you how to increase sales while increasing profit.

How to increase retail sale and profit simultaneously

The 18th century business environment was about speed. The 19th century business environment was about quality. The 21st century business environment is about two things:

- Value
- Total customer experience

What is value?

Value is a quantifiable benefit between both parties involved in a transaction. The key phrase here is: quantifiable benefit. Value has to be sensory specific.

I will further nail down the definition of value with quotes from renowned business experts starting with the Oracle of Omaha, Warren Buffett:

> *"Price is what you pay. Value is what you get."*

Value according to Ron Baker is the amount a customer is willing to pay for a product or service.

> *"Too many people think only of their own profit. But a business opportunity seldom knocks on the door of self-centred people. No customer ever goes to a store merely to please the storekeeper."* Kazuo Inamori, founder of KYOCERA Corp.

> *"The successful producer of an article sells it for more than it cost him to make, and that's his profit. But the customer buys it only because it is worth more to him than he pays for it, and that's his profit. No one can long make a profit producing anything unless the customer makes a profit using it."* Samuel B. Pettengill.

The above quotations by prominent business thinkers were introduced to emphasise the point that for a product or service to be considered valuable, it has to benefit both you and your customers.

What is total customer experience?

Marcus Buckingham in his book "The One Thing You Need to know" wrote that when he interviewed Sir Terry Leahy the man who propelled Tesco into a global brand, he asked him: how he turned Tesco from a UK retailer to the fourth biggest retailer in the world.

Sir Terry told him that when he took over Tesco, the first thing he did was to ask and answer the question: who do we serve?

This question is classic marketing 101: know thy customer.

When they established who they were going to serve, he put in place mechanisms for ensuring they serve their preferred customer. One of those mechanisms they put in place was to increase the numbers of checkout counters in each Tesco store.

When asked why he focused on the checkout counters, he replied with something to the tune of; part of good customer service was to show respect for your customer and what better way of showing respect for someone than showing respect for their time.

21st century retail success therefore, would not be just about the quality of the products you sell or the price you sell them for, but the total customer experience when they visit your store. Total customer experience is your entire package:

- The quality of your products
- The price of your products
- The way your staff interact with the customers
- The way the merchandises are displayed

- Your store design

Below is a list of good customer service quotes that I hope will help you in your journey towards providing total customer experience.

"Do what you do so well that they will want to see it again and bring their friends". Walt Disney.

"It's our job every day to make every important aspect of the customer experience a little bit better." Jeff Bezos, founder of Amazon.

"Your most unhappy customers are your greatest source of learning." Bill Gates, founder of Microsoft.

"There is only one boss. The customer and he can fire everybody in the company from the chairman on down, simply by spending his money somewhere else". Sam Walton, founder of Wal-Mart, the world's largest retailer.

"Customers do you a favour by choosing to do business with you. You aren't doing them a favour by serving them." Mark Sanborn

"If you're not serving the Customer, you'd better be serving someone who is." Jan Carlzon, former president of SAS Airlines

"People will forget what you said. People will forget what you did. But people will never forget how you made them feel." Maya Angelou

"If your business cannot pledge 100% Satisfaction Guaranteed or your money back something is broken. Fix it…No customer walks into your business, gives you money and then says, Dissatisfy me, please. Aim for 100% customer satisfaction…Delivering good customer service is business common sense. Your job is to make it common practice". Bill Quiseng

Retail success fundamentals

In addition to "Level five" leadership and good loss prevention strategy, the key components that have been responsible for the success of a few retail organisations are the following:

- Understanding of their target market
- Trained staff
- Skilled sales staff
- Product knowledge
- Great customer service provision
- Understanding of Their Target Market

I visited Harrods for research about this book and my book on visual merchandise display, Harrods, as previously stated is the Mecca of retailing. Royalty, A-list celebrities and the 'who's who' from around the world fly into London just to shop at Harrods.

You can now imagine my anticipation when I visited Harrods. In my mind everything in Harrods was made of gold. I was disappointed, when I noticed a toy bus I had purchased for my son from ASDA, was also being sold in Harrods.

It was exactly the same toy bus, in exactly the same packaging as the toy in ASDA.

A question popped into my mind, why is it that exactly the same bus, probably manufactured in exactly the same factory in China, is sold in Harrods for twice the price that it is sold for in ASDA?

The answer is decisively simple – ASDA sells a 'toy bus', however, Harrods sells a 'classy toy bus'.

There is a difference.

> *This is marketing 101: people buy emotionally but justify their decision logically.*

Customers who shop at Harrods do not shop there to buy Harrods' products; they shop at Harrods to buy elegance and class. Harrods sells them class even if it is 'Made in China'.

How does Harrods pull this off?

They achieve it with the combination of an elegant store design and attractive visual merchandising displays.

When you move from one department to the next in Harrods, it is like moving from one store to another. Their ability to use their store design to create the illusion of differentiation is one of the keys to Harrods' success.

Harrods understand their customers; they know what their customers desire so they design their store and display their products to satisfy the desire of their customers.

> Tesco serves the ordinary Joe Bloke.
> Wal-Mart serves the person who lives: pay check to pay check.
> The Body Shop serves the ethical consumer.
> Waitrose and Holland & Barrett serve the consumer who wants to live longer.

Ann Summers took merchandise once hidden in secret 'adult' shops; made them chic and took them to the High Street. They made a taboo subject acceptable to the mainstream.

If I was to take my partner shopping at John Lewis, she would probably phone my mother to inform her that I was having a nervous breakdown. She would not want to be caught dead in a John Lewis' outfit. She describes John Lewis' clothing department as a

Bridget Jones museum where they store a collection of Bridget Jones costumes.

However, John Lewis continues to increase profits year on year because John Lewis understands their target market.

Someone like my significant other might not want to be caught dead in John Lewis' outfit, but there are people in the UK, who love Bridget Jones' memorabilia, these people are John Lewis' target market, so John Lewis caters to them.

The most successful retailers understand their target market and show their understanding of their target market through their store design and visual merchandising displays.

On Christmas Eve, I had not done my grocery shopping and was dreading the prospect of entering a supermarket, knowing how packed they were going to be. But as I drove past my local Lidl store, I noticed it was empty. I rushed in and completed my shopping.

As I drove back home a question came to my mind; why is it that even on this day when most supermarkets are typically jam packed was Lidl empty?

The answer is: Lidl does not have a target market. One of their biggest sins was making the decision to force customers to pay for carrier bags. Marks & Spencer can afford to do that because they appeal to a different class of customers.

In Tesco and ASDA, customers who are environmentally conscious have the option of paying for carrier bags. However, those who do not want to pay for carrier bags also have the option of getting free bags.

This is because Tesco and ASDA understand their customers. Lidl's senior management, on the other hand, believed that having implemented a similar strategy in Europe, they could do the same in the UK. If the Brits do not like it, tough! Well, the Brits had shown their displeasure with their feet.

I have used the above examples to demonstrate that success or failure in retail is the result of the strategies every retailer adopts. Those retailers who understand their target market and cater to them will continue to move from success to greater success. Those who roll the dice and hope that customers show up are the ones who will struggle or go into administration.

I hate to be the one breaking this type of news to the retail industry but I guess someone will have to do it: the internet is not going away. This means that retailers are not only competing with one another, they are also competing with factory owners in China whose names they have never heard. Shoppers are now ordering directly from warehouses and distributors, for example an individual can log on to eBay and order a pallet load of goods.

Here is the good news: the majority of people still prefer to shop from physical retail outlets. The question for you is this: how do you ensure that shoppers are attracted to your store?

It can be done by designing your store to take into account their buying habits.

Trained Staff

A friend of mine is a manager at Tesco. He knows the profit margin on each and every product in his store. Why does knowing the profit margins matter for his products?

There are numbers of reasons. Firstly business is about making profit and secondly it highlights the significance of "training" to retail success.

As a manager at Tesco, my friend receives periodic training on every aspect of running a retail business. Little wonder Tesco is the second most profitable retailer in the world and the third most profitable business in the UK.

Tesco, like most successful retailers, understand the significance of staff training to the success of their business. Subsequently, they ensure their staff are constantly trained.

> *It never ceases to amaze me how an individual will open a retail store worth millions of pounds only to have the store managed by someone they are unwilling to spend a few hundred pounds to train.*

The two common excuses retailers give for not training their staff are:

- It is expensive
- Absentee cover

I'm probably the only person who doesn't get it, just imagine this scenario:

Someone, somewhere, is leaving his multi-million pound retail store in the hands of an individual and he says it is too expensive to spend a few hundred pounds to provide that person with the requisite training to manage his store well; can you imagine that?

What am I missing?!

Sales Training

According to a survey commissioned by Blue Martini Software; retailers could be losing up to 85 billion pounds per year as a result of inadequate staff training. The survey revealed that 84% of potential customers who left stores without buying said they were going to buy from another retailer.

This means that the store they entered was unable to sell them on yes, so they sold them on no.

As many as 95% of retail employees have never received any form of sales and marketing training. As a result of their inability to sell, most retail staff just stand by as shoppers examine merchandise and cross their fingers hoping they will decide to buy.

Worst of all are the ones who keep asking the same stupid question for which they know exactly the answer they are going to get: "can I help you?"

"No I am just looking"

Retailing is about selling. This means that anyone in retail should at the very least be given basic sales training.

If retailing is about selling and 95% of retail staff have never received any form of sales training, surely there is a linear relationship between sales training and retail success.

It is like a medical doctor who has never been to medical school, how many people in this world would want an untrained doctor to treat them?

Product Knowledge

Covert sting operations, conducted by 'Which?' the consumer organisation, in 2011, revealed that many retail employees lacked knowledge of the products they sold. Just 8 out of the 154 stores investigated, scored an excellent mark. No well-known High Street brand was amongst those eight.

Surprised?

Maybe not.

In this information age where consumers have access to vast amounts of information one would expect retailers to realise the importance of product knowledge for their staff.

Nowadays, many shoppers search on the internet for products prior to stepping foot in a shop. They read information such as product specification, where to get the best deal and customer reviews. They visit shops to basically clarify what they have already read. If the store staff are unable to answer their questions, there is no chance that they will be able to sell to them.

> Here is the secret, despite the fact that people conduct research on the internet, the large majority still don't trust information found on the internet. That is why books are still highly rated even though the information in most books can be found online.

People still trust other people and prefer to interact with people. This is one reason why despite the internet, bricks and mortar retailing will survive. However, there is a new dynamic and retailers need to understand this.

The consumer of today is better informed than the consumer of ten or twenty years ago. Consequently, today's retail staff need to be better informed than the retail staff of ten or twenty years ago.

> *One cannot navigate the 21st century with a 19th century skill set; it will not work.*

Richer Sounds has been featured in the Guinness Book of Records for the past 20 years as having the highest sales per square foot of any retailer in the world.

Coincidentally, they continue to top the 'Which?' survey for excellent customer service and product knowledge.

Good Customer Service Provision

These days, the only reason I visit my local PC World store is to buy ink for my printer. This is due to the fact that it is the only retailer in my locality that sells the type of ink cartridge suitable for my printer.

Every time I enter a PC World store, I encounter a similar level of service. I am always forced to queue up for a long time at the check-out, waiting for staff to serve me. Even when the store is empty I have to wait to be served, whilst there will be a group of staff chatting a few metres away from the vacant checkout.

PC World and her sister company Curry's are struggling and their management wonder why?

I am sure if they were to go bust the CEO would blame harsh trading conditions. The fact that his store ranks at the bottom of many customer satisfaction surveys would not be seen as a factor in their demise.

In this "Long Tail" retail environment where consumers are constantly presented with endless choices, one would think that retailers, especially High Street retailers would realise the importance of excellent customer service and try to instil it as a fundamental part of their business strategy.

Thirty to 40% of people will buy solely on price. The majority 70% of people will buy on quality and convenience. Even though the retail industry is in crisis, the luxury sector of the industry is still growing strong. This is because no matter what the economic situation is people still shop. The only question is where will they shop.

Luxury retailers understand this fact and train their staff in excellent customer service.

I have noticed in my local ASDA that when staff are asked for information, they do not just point; they take customers to the location and ask them what else they can do for them.

People go to restaurants where the food is terrible but never complain because of the attitude of the staff. However, if it was the other way around, the food tasted great but the service sucked, they are highly unlikely to return to that restaurant.

Good customer service is a key component to the success of many of the most successful retailers whilst bad customer service has been one of the major contributing factors for the failure of many retail ventures.

This is a book about store design, I am sure you would expect me to provide you with tips about designing the physical aspect of your store. So why does it seem as though I am going on about subjects that do not seem related to store design?

The answer is this: store design is about marketing. Remember a business needs five components to succeed:

- Visionary leadership
- Great people
- Good system
- Good marketing system
- Good business model

The life blood of any retail business is its ability to acquire and retain customers. Your success as a retailer will depend on your ability to acquire and retain customers. Your store design is a critical part of your marketing process. Your ability to design your store making use of fundamental business principles will determine your level of success.

One thing you need to understand is, the store design itself is not going to attract customers or increase your sales, your ability to use your store design as a vehicle for the achievement of customer acquisition will be the determining factor.

As stated previously, the likes of Google, Facebook and all of the successful internet entrepreneurs are not successful because of their ability to use the internet better than the rest of us. They are successful because of their ability to effectively use the internet as a tool through which they can apply fundamental business principles.

> In Value Migration, Adrian Slywotzky stated that *"A business (model) design is the totality of how a company selects its customers, defines and differentiates its offerings (or responses), defines the tasks it will perform itself and those it will outsource; configures its resources; goes to market; creates utility for customers and captures profits. It is the entire system for delivering utility to customers and earning a profit from that activity"*.

In their paper *"while the term 'business model' is often used these days, it is seldom defined explicitly."* Chesbrough and Rosenbloom point out that there are six specific functions of a business model:

- Articulate the value proposition – the value created to users by using the product.
- Identify the market segment – to whom and for what purpose is the product useful; specify how revenue is generated by the firm.
- Define the value chain – the sequence of activities and information required to allow a company to design, produce, market, deliver and support its product or service.
- Estimate the cost structure and profit potential – using the value chain and value proposition identified.

- Describe the position of the firm with the value network – link suppliers, customers, counterparts and competitors.
- Formulate the competitive strategy – how will you gain and hold your competitive advantage over competitors or potential new entrants.

Joan Magretta wrote in the Harvard Business Review in May 2002: *"A good business model answers Peter Drucker's age-old questions: "Who is the customer?" And "what does the customer value?" It also answers the fundamental questions every manager must ask: How do we make money in this business? What is the underlying economic logic that explains how we can deliver value to customers at an appropriate cost"?*

Your retail store is first and foremost a business and like any business it is dependent on your marketing process – your ability to acquire and retain customers; the extent to which you are capable of marketing your retail store with an attractive store design that is focused on providing value and total customer experience, will be the extent to which you are going to succeed.

Incidentally while writing this chapter; I took a break to relax. I switched on the television. BBC Click was on. The program was about new types of buildings that respond to the movement of people.

Just like the new great buildings that are being constructed to generate energy automatically, the building will be capable of changing in relation to the movement of people. Even a chair will adjust itself to suit the shape of the person sitting on it.

In short, buildings of the future are going to be designed on functionality. The question that this brings to mind is: How functional is your retail store?

Is your store designed for the customers of two decades ago or is it designed for customers of the next two decades?

Let me provide you a few tips on how to design a retail store that results in increased sales:

Step 1:
Identify your target market.

Step 2:
Find out what factors influence their buying behaviour.

Step 3:
Focus your store design exclusively on satisfying the desires and buying behaviours of your target market.

Step 4:
Choose colour schemes, fixtures, fittings, display space, location of cashier counter, location of customer services desk, shelf height, in accordance with the findings made in your target market research.

Step 5:
Incorporate the security of your merchandise into your store design. This is the most important aspect of the store design as stores need to be designed in such a way that they design-out crime. (Whether it is employee theft or shoplifting; a well-designed store can effectively design out crime.)

Step 6:
Take the effective use of technology into account when designing your store. Whether it is a POS, CCTV or EBR system they all need to be included in the design blueprint. A good POS system can rapidly increase sales by reducing queues. CCTV and EBR systems reduce crime whether shoplifting or employee theft.

Chapter Three

How to Increase Retail Sales With Brand Image Selling

There is more to retailing than merchandise and selling. It is also about your customers' perception of your brand and what it represents. Their perception and the connection they make with your brand and what it represents is the most important component of your marketing strategy.

Retail business is like showbiz. It is all about image, brand and style. Many people choose to work in a particular business, not because of the financial reward they hope to gain, but the value the business represents.

> Most people associate The Body Shop with ethics.
> Harrods is perceived as elegant and classy.
> Victoria's Secret is the lovers' choice for lingerie.

Customers who shop at The Body Shop do so largely because their products are not tested on animals. They also feel that by purchasing The Body Shop products they are swaying their conscience.

Harrods markets itself as an elegant store that attracts classy people. Royalties the world over, Hollywood 'A' list stars and the 'who is who' in the world go to London specifically to shop at Harrods, all because it has created an image of elegance.

Victoria's Secret is the preferred choice for ladies shopping for lingerie for that special occasion. In the minds of most of them, Victoria's Secret has come to represent love. When women want to go on a special date or when they want to surprise their significant other, they shop for their special bedroom lingerie at Victoria's Secret. Wearing lingerie from Victoria's Secret gives them confidence.

These retailers have carved a place in the hearts of shoppers by getting them to link their brand with their image. The image cultivated by those brands has been responsible for their phenomenal success in the retail industry.

Image selling is vital for the success of any retail venture, without it most retail businesses struggle. Image selling is a very effective sales strategy and used properly, it can make the selling process very easy.

The crux of image selling is twofold:

- The image that the customer wants to portray by purchasing your merchandise
- The image that the customer already knows that your store represents

A person willing to spend a quarter of a million pounds to buy a Ferrari is not doing so simply because he wants to drive a fast car. He chose to buy a Ferrari because of the prestige associated with owning a Ferrari.

Every person deep down wants recognition and the appreciation of others. Shrewd marketers tap into the human desire for recognition and craft their marketing messages to fulfil that desire.

In his book "Breakthrough Advertising" Eugene Schwartz describes this human behaviour as identification. He defined identification as:

> "the desire of a person to act a certain role in their lives and to define himself to the world around him—to express the qualities within himself that he values and the position he has attained. All products may benefit from the power to define. But in particular,

when you have a product that does the same job as competing products, and is so priced that price is no longer a factor then expect choice will almost overwhelmingly depend on the difference in role that your product offers him".

I once watched an interview with a Ferrari executive. He let it be known that when you drive a Ferrari, you drive a dream.

This statement is so true.

Most men who are into cars view Ferrari as the ultimate driving machine. Although it is not the most expensive car in the world, driving a Ferrari is like a dream come true for many people.

As you design your store you need to be considering the roles and characteristics you want your customers to associate it with. Whatever role and characteristic you choose must be one they already possess in their head. You cannot invent a role or characteristic from thin air.

Remember? Driving a Ferrari is driving a dream.

Going into your retail store is what…Complete the sentence.

I attended a business start-up event in London and met a few retail businesses. When I interviewed the retailers at the stands about what made their products different from those of the other retailers in the arena, not a single one could tell me any differentiating factor. They all said their products were made specifically for the consumer et cetera, et cetera.

I kept priming them to see if at least one could come up with anything that was closely relate to the benefit the customer will derive from purchasing their products. Not a single one was able to come up with the benefit of their products to their customers.

A prerequisite for success in the retail industry or in any business for that matter is the ability to differentiate your business from that of the competition.

The second aspect of image selling is the association you want your customers to have with your brand.

Image selling is the ability to market an idea that people cling to, that which in the end creates a positive perception in their mind about your brand.

Certain brands are associated with ethics, healthy lifestyle, elegance, class, low quality, safety, innocence or quality.

However, to sell an image effectively, the image has to be implanted in the minds of your customers from the start of your business.

Certain retail organisations have been trying to flaunt their Green credentials by selling carrier bags. Although they might be honestly doing it for environmental reasons, the fact that they had not done it from their formative stages leads most people to think they are just doing it as an excuse to increase their profit margin.

Europe based supermarkets such as ALDI and LiDL operating in the UK and US charge for carrier bags. However, they have been doing so from the start of their operations in those countries, even though other retailers give carrier bags for free. Therefore, no one will accuse them of charging for carrier bags to increase profit.

The image your retail organisation projects could be that of the philosophy of the founder. Your organisation could represent *fun, love or passion for life*.

It really does not matter what image you choose to project. What is important is your brand is associated with something. To maintain that image, your store and entire work environment should reflect that image.

For example, if the image you want to project is that of a fun-loving organisation, your store colours should be bright and it should be designed to be cheery.

If you want to project the image of an environmentally conscious organisation; then your store colour should be green and it should be designed so that all of your fixtures are made from recyclable materials.

However, your brand image is not just your logo, colour or store design. It is also your brand promise. It is what customers can expect when they interact with your brand. A good brand image is part and parcel of the retail success secret of successful retailers and is a very effective marketing tool utilised with laser accuracy by those retailers.

Although image is intangible; it is more valuable than the products in your store.

Just the Logo of multinational corporations such as Coca Cola, Nike, Google and Apple carry a value many times that of some developing countries. Those multinationals spare no effort because they know that brand sells the products not the other way round.

- Nike represents hero
- Timberland represents adventure
- Rolex represents luxury
- Why is image and branding so important for store design?

Branding and image is important because they are the information upon which the store design blueprint is based. When customers enter your store, they need to be able to connect to your brand image inside the store.

Your brand image is an implicit promise to your customers about who you are and what you represent, consequently it is essential that you jealously protect and promote your image.

Store design fundamentals

> *"So with any other mail order ad which has long continued. Every feature, every word and picture teaches advertising at its best. You may not like them. You may say they are unattractive, crowded, hard to read — anything you will. But the test of results has proved those ads the best salesman those lines have yet discovered. And they certainly pay"* (Claude C. Hopkins – Scientific Advertising).

The above summarises the concept of creating a marketing design. Most retailers have not connected their store design with their marketing strategies so they leave the design of the store to store fitters with no knowledge about marketing or advertising.

As I previously pointed out the difference between someone passing by your store in a busy shopping centre and entering your store, rests upon your store design.

Most designers equate beauty with good design. The aim of a marketing design is not to impress customers with beauty. It is to enhance your marketing message. Some marketing designs don't work because those creating the design do not understand the fundamentals of marketing design.

Most designers think that it is about adding fancy images to a design to make it look fanciful. Fanciful designs are good for comics and children's' books. In the marketing world it is about the message.

Every component of the design has to serve the purpose of enhancing the core marketing message, not distract from it.

The one thing that should be uppermost in your mind when it comes to marketing design is simplicity. Most Apple products are not the best designed products in the world. However, they outsell all products in their niche.

Why, because Apple focuses on *simplicity, elegance and functionality*.

Their products are functional and elegant.

Google website is one of the top five high traffic websites in the world. Yet the Google home page is just the Google logo, and a few tabs at the top.

Look at ads in the top selling newspapers and magazines. You will notice that they are mostly in black and white and most of them have no images, only essential information relating to the product or service.

When the London 2012 logo was unveiled, no one except the designers seemed to know what they had designed. Some people described it as a child's drawing. Some say it symbolised an angry reaction.

It was call various things, but a reference to the Olympics. The chairman of the London organising Olympic committee had to go on television to explain to the British public what the logo meant.

> *When a logo is designed for an event as popular as the Olympics and no one understands the design, there is a serious design fault.*

Figure 8: London 2012 Olympic logo confused everyone

This is a lesson for you. Pay attention. As you create your store design you need to ensure that the design is clearly understood by your target market and that it appeals to them.

The goal of your store design has to be:

- Simplicity
- Functionality
- Clarity

Why do most advertising fail?

"Some ads are planned and written with some utterly wrong conception. They are written to please the seller. The interests of the buyer are forgotten. But one can never sell goods profitably, in person or in print, when that attitude exists" (Claude C. Hopkins – Scientific Advertising).

Although store design is advertisement, many store designs fail to attract customers for the same reasons that many advertisements fail to attract customers' attention.

Look at your current store design and ask yourself the following questions:

- Was it designed with the customer in mind?
- Does your store fit with your customer avatar?

- Did you take into account your competition?
- Is your store design simple, functional and clear?
- Does your store design represent your core message?

If you cannot answer all the above questions in the affirmative, you will want to reconsider your current store design.

How to design a store that represents your brand image

The following steps are effective for creating your image:

Step 1:
Identify the image you want to be associated with. It can either be the philosophy of the founder or the organisation as a whole. It first needs to be identified along with the story of why you want to be associated with that particular image.

Step 2:
Communicate that image to your store designer in order for it to be incorporated into the store design blueprint.

Step 3:
Design your store to reflect that image. Every fixture, lighting and decor in the store needs to be congruent with that image.

Step 4:
Ensure all store assistants are well briefed and up to speed on your brand image. Their uniforms, actions and interaction with customers need to reflect your projected image.

The main point to remember here is that as powerful as image selling is, it is a process. It is not an event. It is a process that needs to be consciously built into your marketing strategy and plan from your formative stages.

What is Brand Image?

The most successful retailers have carved out an image that the buying public can easily associate them with.

How to Market Your Brand Image?

Steps for Marketing Your Brand Image

The following steps will help you to effectively market your image:

Step 1:

Identify your desired brand image. You need to have a mission and value statement that articulates what you stand for. It must also contain information about why you stand for that.

Step 2:

Ensure your store designers fully understand the image you want to project to your customers in order for every aspect of it to be incorporated into your store design blueprint.

Step 3:

Ensure your store is designed in congruence with your desired image.

Step 4:

Ensure all employees within your organisation are aware of your brand image and adhere to it in every aspect of their job.

Your brand image is the most valuable asset in your retail organisation, it is an intangible asset. A good image can make you successful. A negative image will cause you to fail, so build and guard your image and ensure that the message of your image is communicated to your store designers.

Chapter Four

Designing Store For Increase Customer Flow

In chapter one, I mentioned two retailers from different spectrum of the retail success continuum: Harrods one of the most successful retailers in the world and Early Learning Centre a struggling UK retailer.

They both sell children's toys.

In Harrods children are able to play with the toys in the store strategically stimulating an attachment to the toys that results in them pressurising their parents to buy it for them.

While the Early Learning Centre has a Soviet style dental suite store where children cannot even breathe or walk around without stepping on each other's toes and parents have to stay outside of the store when their children are inside.

Increasing retail sales requires four core elements

- Attracting customers as they pass by the store
- Enticing them to enter the store
- Retaining them longer in the store
- Persuading them to buy

There is not a single one of these four core elements that one would stand out as a single factor that on its own can result in increased sales. However, if it is a case of being forced to choose one from four, I will say retaining customers in the store would be the most important of the four. This is because the longer customers stay in the store, more likely they are to buy.

To hold customers in your store for a long time, they need to be able to move freely within the store without any form of hindrance. A retail store has three basic design components:

1) Selling area
2) Services area
3) Circulation area

The extent to which these areas are effectively utilised, especially the selling area will have an effect on the success of the retailer.

Shopping is a favoured pastime for many people. For a great many people shopping is a necessity. However, in a majority of the cases, recreational shopping is more prevalent than shopping out of necessity. Visit any city centre at the weekend and you will notice the High Street jam packed with shoppers. Despite the hoard of people in the city centre, as you walk around, you will notice some packed and empty stores.

Have you ever wondered why this is the case?

The reason for this is that for most people the act of going to shopping is an event. Those who buy for recreational purposes do not go shopping just to buy things. They love the experience. There might be ten thousand people in the city centre on a particular day, but each one of them has a personal reason for being in the city.

The stores that attract the most customers are those that appeal to the reasons for those people being in the city centre. 21st century retailing is not about buying and selling, it is also about the experience that customers have in the process; it is about the atmosphere in the store and how comfortable customers feel in it.

Starbucks sells coffee like many other coffee shops, yet people prefer Starbucks to other coffee shops. Starbucks does not sell some types of technologically advanced coffee that is proven to give long life, yet customers prefer Starbucks over other Cafes.

This is due to the fact that Starbucks creates an environment in which customers feel relaxed and comfortable. When customers feel this way they are more inclined to purchase more coffee. A similar principle applies to your retail store. It must be a place where customers will not only come to buy what they need but also somewhere that they like to relax.

An Apple store in a shopping centre is always full of people. Even in the middle of the day when most retail stores are empty, Apple stores are buzzing with people. The reason for that, Apple stores are cool places to be.

Many people make buying decisions in the store after they have had the time to browse the merchandises. You want your customers spending their time buying, and not waste time navigating clutter.

The goal of any retail store is to attract customers and then persuade them to buy. Good advertising and promotion works to bring customers into the store. But when they are in the store, their decision to buy could be down to the layout and design. Both play a huge role in how customers rate their experiences, whether they buy and if they return or recommend the store to others.

Think about the experience you want to create for customers who enter your store. Picture the type of store design that would make it possible for customers to move from the front to the rear of the store browsing products and how they will go to the checkout counter without encountering obstacles.

Another important element in customer flow is the interaction of your store's sales assistants with customers:

When customers enter your store, how are they greeted?

When they need help, are store associates ready to assist them?

Are they trained to provide answers to the costumers' questions?

I know a sports retailer in the UK that spends millions advertising in prime locations all around the country. However, when customers visit their stores, there are never enough store associates to serve them and when they have a question; the store associates haven't a clue.

How do you display high-value and impulse items?

Do you strategically locate high-value and impulse products?

Take some time to strategically locate high ticket items. It will determine your level of sales of those items. One objective of your store design should be to create a space where customers and sales associates can move freely, maximize space and make the most of your product exposure.

What is customer flow?

Customer flow in a retail environment refers to the manner in which customers move from the point of entry into the store until they leave the store. Customer flow refers to the ease with which customers walk through the aisles; many ways in which they gain access to products, sample products, have their questions answered and ease with which they pay for products and exit the store.

A good customer flow system should respond to customer's choice. The customer should have visible options. These ought to include easy access to products and customer service that results in positive impression of your store.

In a retail environment where the entire operation depends on various actors and factors, customer flow doesn't just happen. It must be purposely created as a part of your store design blueprint; managed and continuously improved to take into account the changing retail environment.

Store design plays a key part in relation to customer flow because the design of the store facilitates easy movement of your customers from end to end.

Your store is a stage for your brand; a display case for your products and an exceptional three-dimensional experience for your customers. The design, style and finish of your store will have a powerful, lasting impact on customer loyalty and purchasing decisions.

Aisle signage and shelf labelling form another part of your customer flow plan. Throughout the store signage and labelling should be set to enable customers locate products easily and familiarise themselves with the store layout.

You might want to consider seasonal themes. In summer you can create tropical scenery to lure customers to an area in the store where they can view related products and so on.

What are the various types of store design?

Listed below are the three basic types of store designs that encourage customer flow:

Free flow design

The Free flow design system allows products to be arranged throughout the store. Use racks and shelves that enable customers to browse freely with store associates on hand and ready to provide assistance when necessary.

A free flow store design is mainly used in boutiques, clothing, jewellery, and specialty stores. The cons of this design is: if display racks and products are not well arranged the store can appear cluttered and difficult for customers to navigate.

Grid pattern design

The Grid pattern design is usually used by drugstores, supermarkets and superstores. Mostly used in a rigid retail environment that offers less flexibility and encourages customers to search for items on their own.

But a grid pattern layout requires multiple rows filled with a variety of products throughout the store. High ticket items are displayed in high traffic locations and end caps so the customer can't help but notice them.

Such locations also support impulse buying. With a Grid pattern design customers are only able to familiarise themselves with the store layout and location of products after repeated visits.

Spine design

The spine design contains elements of the free flow and grid pattern store design. It is the third most commonly used retail store design strategy. It has a single long main aisle that goes from the entrance of the store to the back of the store. With the spine design, products can be displayed on both sides of the aisle using either the free flow or grid layout or a combination of the two. This design is mostly favoured by department stores because of the different range of products they display.

How to use store design to increase customer flow

A research into customer flow in the UK revealed that 75% of customers only saw a maximum of 25% of products on display in a retail store.

Just pause and think for a moment!

What will happen to your sales if your customers saw at a glance, all of the products on display in your store.

Your objective should be to design your store in such a way that it leads customers around the store. Furthermore, the aim has to be to create a design that ensures they are purposefully directed around the store instead of walking aimlessly around.

To use this analogy, you are designing a racetrack and not a runway. A racetrack design encourages customers to go around the store and be exposed to all the products in the store, whilst a runway encourages customer to move up and down the store in high speed.

Here now are some tips on designing your store to increase customer flow:

Positioning your checkout counters

The position of checkout counters is critical for controlling the movement of customers in your store. Generally customers walk away from checkout counters because checkout counters remind them that they are going to spend money.

Therefore, it is crucial that you position the checkout counter in such a way that it is not the first thing customers see when they enter the store. After they are relaxed, they will naturally gravitate towards it. The right positioning of your checkout counter can result in increased sales.

Control customer movement

You are designing to encourage customer movement around the store. To achieve this; products need to be strategically displayed to persuade shoppers to move from one end to the next and in the process view other products. The way to ensure this is to place essential products in different locations of the store.

Especially essential products such as:

- Milk
- Bread
- Sugar
- Toilet paper
- Detergent
- Coffee
- Beverages

Strategically locate these products around your store in order to force customers to walk around in search of them.

Make adequate use of sightlines

Sightlines are a very critical component for encouraging customer flow. They attract customer's attention as they move around the store and they generate curiosity. Strategically locating sightlines in your store would encourage customers to move around and get to know what products are on display.

Create destination departments

There needs to be destination departments in key locations of your store and ensure customers are aware of them. They need to be strategically located close to the entrance and exit points and in high traffic areas of the store.

Examples of such departments may be:

- The Power Tool Department
- The Seedling or Bedding Plants department
- The Ski Department

- The In-house Deli
- Lighting
- Shoe
- Electronics
- Technology

Use the right lighting system

At all times your customers need to be able to easily see as they walk around the store. Product areas need to be properly lit to attract their attention. When customers feel trapped or lost in your store they will leave immediately.

Create narrow aisles

Create narrow aisle space that would slow down customers as they walk around your store and get them to look at more products. However, the aisles have to be wide enough for the comfort of the customer. Wide aisle space encourages customers to move fast through them without actually browsing the products especially if they already know what they want to buy.

Strategically locate high demand products

High demand merchandise needs to be located at the end of the aisles. This encourages customers to walk pass other products before getting to them.

Display impulse items strategically

Display impulse buys, small and constantly in need and regularly purchased products close to checkout counter and in high traffic areas.

Strategically locate promotional products

Feature or promotional products should never be placed at the entrance to your store. When customers enter your store, they need time to adjust to the environment. They are less likely to pay careful attention to products that they see as they enter.

Do not neglect disabled customers

When designing your store, consideration has to be made for customers with disabilities and special needs. Aisles need to be wide enough to accommodate wheelchairs or mother with prams.

A successful retail store design strategy creates a store that leaves your customers with a happy experience. However it is essential that you regularly refresh your design to take into account and reflect changing trends.

Your store associates can play an important role in increasing customer flow and enhancing your customer experience. The quality of service and experience your customers receive will result in return customers.

Chapter Five

How To Choose Your Store Colour And Layout

Design is the most important aspect of a store layout. When the design is poor, the shopping experience of the customer can be ruined resulting in complaints and eventually loss of customers. The key to a workable design that attracts customers to your store is to determine the total customer experience you wish to achieve.

The appearance of a store is often fundamental to the success of that store. The most successful retailers maintain a consistent layout, colour scheme and other thematic elements that help customers recognise the organisation.

The colour and layout of a retail store can be the difference between a great shopping experience and one that results in a shopper exiting your store empty-handed.

In many stores, customers are unable to touch products that are in packaging. As a part of your store strategy, you need to think of ways of creating an interactive layout that provides customers an opportunity to have a feel of the products.

One way would be to display models of the products as was discussed in the case of Harrods' children section, to allow customers the opportunity of sampling products. An example will be to place batteries in electronic devices so that customers are able to sample them. This strategy alone can dramatically increase your sales.

A good store layout will not only help you influence customer's behaviour by properly designing customer flow, merchandise placement and the entire ambiance; it also provides you with an understanding of sale per square foot. This can help you properly determine the extent to which you are utilising your selling space.

Below is a breakdown of the benefits of having good store layout.

Layout your image

Your store is not only the theatre for the physical display of your products. It is also an outline of the image of your store. Like any business, image sells and your store image is more valuable than your merchandise. Having the right layout can enhance your overall image.

Predict customer buying behaviour

The strategic arrangement of fixtures, strategic placement of staircases, escalators and departments affect store traffic and the amount of time customers spend in your store. The longer customers stay in your store, the more likely is it that they will buy. Therefore, the goal of your store layout needs to be to keep customers as long as possible in your store.

A good example of strategically laying out a retail store to retain customers for longer in the store is the display strategy used by supermarkets and grocery retailers. They display essential products such as bread, milk and egg at the end of the store.

It forces customers to walk pass other products before reaching them. Department stores also use this strategy. By placing children department on the top floor of their store, they encourage customers to walk through other departments thus increasing the possibility of them buying other things as they walk.

Maximize selling space

You can measure the productivity of your sales space per square foot by monitoring the sales figure of each area in your store. Based on your assessment of the outcome of your measurement, if you notice that a specific area of the store is not meeting its sales goals, you can rearrange the fixtures and merchandises to improve the situation.

The objective of an effective store layout is to display as much merchandise as possible per square foot and ensure the merchandise is displayed to attract sales.

Ensure high value items are given priority when designing your store layout. Low ticket items can be displayed in such a way as to ensure they occupy minimum space.

Implement contextual display

The implementation of a contextual display is another way of making effective use of your display space. Products that are somewhat related to one another can be displayed in the same location. This is likely to trigger impulse buying and maximise the use of your selling space.

Also placing similar brands in the same section or displaying complementary products such as shirts and ties increases the possibility of sales and is a good use of display space.

Use layout to instigate positive emotions

Your store layout can determine the customer's emotion and sentiment they display while they are in your store. The emotions your store layout triggers in customers as they walk around would determine whether they buy or not.

If you intend to trigger a positive and relaxed feeling, your choice of colour, the arrangement of the merchandise and fixtures would determine whether you trigger your desired emotion in the customer.

Loss prevention

In the final analysis, your ultimate desire is to make a profit. The best way of making profit is to increase sales and reduce shrinkage. Creative arrangement of your merchandises, fixtures and layout can reduce the possibility of crime in your store.

The manner, in which your store is laid out, sends a signal to criminals, dishonest employees or shoplifters that you will not tolerate any form of criminal activity. It is very critical that you involve loss prevention in the preparation of your store design blueprint. By including loss prevention in the process you can benefit from expert advice on how to use your store layout to design out crime.

The importance of colour in store design

Colour is a very critical aspect of your store design. Colour is a very powerful intangible aspect of a design that if used properly can result in enormous benefit for the store.

On the other hand executed poorly, it can result in loss sales. Colour has a huge effect on the mood of people. Colour can stimulate happiness, relaxation, a feeling of comfort or it can result in anxiety and restlessness.

Consequently, as you make the decision on the colour of your store, the deciding factor has to be what emotion you want to trigger in your customers. Choosing a colour scheme to distinguish your store from the competition is somewhat of an art and a science, and it depends on your type of retail store and the image you wish to convey.

There are a lot of guidelines regarding colour application. For instance dark colour is inappropriate for small spaces or painting a space white makes it appear larger and grander.

Imagine how inviting your store would look with professionally painted signs, texture effects and the latest paint finishes. Or a super-modern digital print hangings, stencilled designs and murals that create a striking feature that will attract new customers to your store.

Colours such as blue, purple, white and green are believed to encourage a feeling of calm and relaxation. It is believed that stores decorated with these colours stimulate a feeling of rationalisation and positive thoughts in the minds of customers, resulting in them spending more in those stores.

Customers in stores with those colours are generally calmer, go about their shopping slowly and stay longer in the store.

On the other hand, stores with red or orange considered hot colours generate a feeling of anxiety and claustrophobia in their customers. Customers in those stores do not stay long because they feel uneasy, restless and impatient.

However, all colours have their pros and cons. Bright colours such as red and orange are excellent colours for attracting attention to your store. In most instances, the first thing a customer notices when on a shopping spree is not the name of the retailer or its brand logo but its colour.

How to determine a good colour and store layout?

Listed below are steps for determining your store's colour and layout:

Step One

It is very critical that every aspect of your store layout is taken into consideration during the planning stage of your store design. The essence of the layout is to reflect your store's image; therefore it has to be part and parcel of your store design blueprint.

Step Two

Decide on the type of atmosphere you want to have in your store. You might prefer your store to look feminine, sophisticated, masculine, child friendly, gothic or unisex.

Step Three

Choose the appropriate colour scheme for your target market. If your store is a lingerie store, you might want to go for a sultry, sensual feel. This would demand using colours such as black, cream, gold, deep pink and red, as opposed to blue, green or yellow.

When choosing walls and flooring colours, it is very important to keep the goal of the space usage in mind. If you intend on selling children products, warm and exhilarating colours would be appropriate.

Step Four

Offer multiple buying opportunities when customers are in your store. Create your design blueprint in a way that popular items are placed at the back of the store to ensure customers walk through the entire store. Display inexpensive and impulse items at the front of the store or close to the checkout counter.

Step Five

Make your store as easy as possible to navigate by placing clear signs in each section. Ensure products are accessible by using fixtures that are easy for customers to reach. When customers are unable to reach products, they might just leave without buying.

Step Four

Ensure you have adequate space for customers to walk freely across aisles. Narrow aisles create a feeling of entrapment. The front of the store should be more spacious than other areas because that is the where the highest level of traffic is located.

Step Five

Ensure high ticket items are displayed in secured cabinets to reduce the risk of theft. When customers want to see those items, a staff member should be available to open the cabinet for them.

Step Six

Select the appropriate lighting system. Store lighting systems would be dealt with in another chapter. However, it is important that you include the lighting system in your store design layout because light plays a crucial role in product presentation. A good lighting system can make a product appear more valuable than it actually is.

The layout and design you chose for your store needs to be based on the overall vision of your store. You first and foremost need to take into account your target market. It is the selection of your target market that would determine the type of layout and colour that would suit your store.

Chapter Six

The Best Retail Store Lighting System

Retailers tend to focus on ample lighting while paying scant attention to the quality of the light in their store. But the quality of light in your store is a very significant determinant of the success of your store. Good lighting is important for:

- Attracting customers into your store
- Guiding them through the store
- Helping them evaluate the products
- Helping your store associates complete sale swiftly and accurately

More than the above light is closely linked to:

- Increasing store sales
- Providing customers with a good impression of your type of store
- Increasing the perceived value of your products
- Creating a conducive shopping environment for your customers

The most common things taken into consideration whenever retailers think of ways of increasing sales are:

a) Increased advertising
b) Intensive promotion
c) New product line
d) Changing store fixtures

e) Relocating products

The lighting scheme of their store is never taken into consideration. A good quality lighting system in your store enhances the look of both the store and the display.

When your store appearance is enhanced because of good lighting customers are more likely to believe that the products in your store are of high quality. The core of marketing is perception…what the customer thinks about your store.

I am not suggesting you deceive your customers with lighting technology. What I am trying to point out is that good lighting increases the chances of customers wanting to enter your store.

Listed below are the most commonly used retail lighting systems:

Ambient Lighting

Figure 9: Ambient lighting aid shoppers movement around the store

Ambient lighting is the basic lighting system in a retail store that aids customers' movement around the store and helps them to evaluate products. Ambient lighting is just a basic lighting system; light that enables people to see clearly when they get on with mundane activity in a slightly dark area.

Accent Lighting

Figure 10: Accent Lighting is used to highlight a specific item in a displace

Accent lighting commonly known as "focus" lighting is used to draw attention to a few products in a retail store. This is particularly useful for highlighting high ticket or promotional products.

Accent lighting is the favoured lighting system of luxury retailers. That's because it allows them to highlight individual products in the store. Except for promotion accent lighting is not very useful in a low end store.

High Activity Lighting

Figure 11: High Activity Lighting focuses attention on a specific department

High Activity Lighting schemes are used to focus attention on a particular area of the store. Whilst accent light focuses on a specific product, High Activity Lights focus on specific areas. There might be areas of the store that are darker because of location or fixtures. High Activity Lights can be used to brighten up such areas.

High Activity Lights can also be used to promote a certain department or section of the store. If there is less traffic in certain areas of the store, High Activity Lights can be used to increase traffic to those areas by highlighting them.

Shelf and Case Lighting

Figure 12: Shelf and Case Lighting is used to illuminate display cabinet

Shelf and Case Lightings are used in display cabinets and shelves where certain high ticket or exclusive items are displayed. Shelf and Case Lighting serves two purposes: to ensure that the product is properly seen in the display case and to enhance the appearance of the product.

Perimeter and Valance Lighting

Figure 13: Perimeter and Valance Lighting is used for towers and tall shelves

The Perimeter lighting scheme is used for tall vertical shelving and displays. While a valance lighting scheme conceals the source of light on merchandise. Perimeter lights are often positioned in a way that they illuminate the vertical surfaces of the area.

Architectural Lighting

Figure 14: Architectural lighting highlights the design of a building

The Architectural lighting scheme is used to light up and highlight the architectural design of a building. Architectural lighting can be used on the inside or outside of a building. Luxury retailers use Architectural lighting to show up the shape of their retail design.

Task Lighting

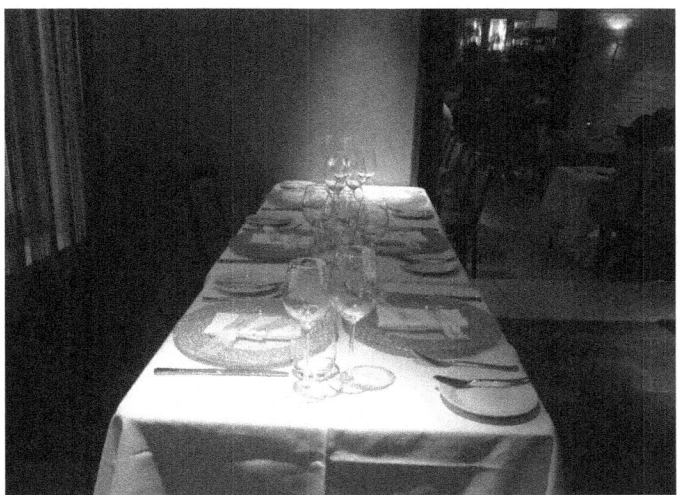

Figure 15: Task Lighting is used to conduct specific task

Task lights are installed specifically for use by staff assigned to specific tasks. They can be installed at the checkout counter, customer services counter or in specific areas of the store where store associates are expected to perform specific tasks.

Your lighting scheme needs to help customers to see what you sell and your store associates perform their duties well.

Be aware that Illumination of your store is a major factor in your customer's buying decision. In most instances shoppers will not buy a product if they have not had the opportunity to properly evaluate it and establish its specific attributes such as colour, texture and quality.

Your store lighting must also be good enough for customers to be able to read the price tag and labels of products.

Generally, a good lighting level in a store is about 75 foot candle and a bit higher level if your target market is older people.

The decision as to which lighting system you choose for your store should be guided by the primary objectives of any retail lighting system:

Attracting customers into your store

The style of lighting you have in your store should signal to your customers that your store is open for business. Your lighting system needs to breed curiosity in shoppers as they pass by your store.

Guide them through the store

You lighting needs to guide customers around the store and to specific areas you would like them to see. When you make effective use of accent lighting, you can control customers' movement within the store and persuade them to go from one section to the next to see what's on display.

Helping the customers evaluate the products

An adequately lit area makes it easier for customers to weigh up products and make buying decisions. When customers have the opportunity to checkout products without any form of hindrance, they are more likely to make a buying decision.

Helping your store associates complete sale swiftly and accurately

The point-of-sale, customer service desk, changing rooms and all other points of the store where store associates are expected to serve customers, need to be well lit so they could perform their duties easily.

Below are some important factors to consider when installing lighting system in your store:

- Colour rendering index/colour temperature

- Contrast/accent/highlight
- Daylight Integration/regulator
- Direct glare/reflected glare
- Image/style
- Modelling of objects/shadows
- Visual priority/organization
- Quantity of light on vertical displays
- Quantity of light on horizontal surfaces
- Use high colour rendering lights

When selecting your lighting system, you need to ensure that the types of bulbs you choose are those that make product colours appear as natural as possible.

What to look for when selecting your light system?

The specification on the packaging that indicates it renders colours accurately.

Colour rendering index (CRI) is specified on bulb packaging or on manufacturer's catalogues.

CRI of lights ranges from one to as high as a hundred. For your store, you need to select lights with a CRI of 80 or above. Some standard halogen incandescent, fluorescent and metal halide lights meet the 80 and above CRI value.

Lighting fixtures should limit glare

Ensure that the type of lighting system you choose limit the customer's view of the light louvers, baffles, and lenses. When light shines in the eyes of the customer, it creates discomfort and reduces the customer's desire to stay in your store.

Lighting system such as accent Lighting should be aimed directly at the products. Spot lights with small beams should be selected as well as fixtures in which the light is dipped into the fixture's opening. Ensure that lights are not aimed directly toward the aisles or doorways to prevent it shining into the eyes on customers.

Properly distribute light

Light has to be evenly distributed throughout your store. The entrance, areas between aisles and display have to be well lit to ensure customers are able to see products properly as they move around the store.

Since most products are displayed vertically, it is essential that the lighting system you select can properly light vertical surfaces. This is possible by using adjustable fixtures that can be directed toward shelves and vertical displays or by selecting ceiling-mounted fixtures that are designed for all round coverage.

Attract customers to products with light

Figure 16: A good lighting system makes products appear more attractive and valuable

A good lighting system can be an effective way of attracting customer's attention to specific areas of your store you would like them to go.

It is a mistake to use spot or accent Light such as halogen reflector lamps all over your store. They make the store appear cluttered and can sometimes confuse the customers. Light should be effectively used to attract customers and adequate in specific areas such as checkout or customer service counters.

Below is a further guide for choosing and implementing an effective lighting system:

> Place the lighting source as close as possible to the merchandise.
>
> For ambient lighting, use efficient diffusers such as fluorescents.
>
> For accent lighting, use narrow beam spotlights such as Halogen PARs or Low-Voltage MR-16s.
>
> Brighten up your store aisles with spill light from the accented merchandising areas or displays.
>
> Use the lightest colours on the interior surfaces of shelving.
>
> Ensure you use organized patterns of lighting fixtures. Chaotic patterns may confuse, agitate or fatigue the customers.
>
> Ensure you use high colour rendering lamps for both ambient and task lighting

In clothing stores the lights must be adequate in sales areas and dressing rooms so that customers can see how the items look prior to purchasing.

While lighting must attract customers to your store, the objective needs to be to enable customers to read signage and move unhindered throughout the store. The level and quality of the illumination in your store will create a lasting impression on your customers and will be the key to whether they will return to your store.

Be aware that the lighting system is as dynamic as the products you display; therefore you cannot be rigid about it. You need to understand that certain displays and seasons might require a different lighting system.

Consequently, it is extremely important that you ensure that your store designers make provisions for such events.

Chapter Seven

How To Wow Customers With Creative Storefront Design

As a part of my research for this book, I stopped in at shopping centres around the UK. That was in January, one of the most important months in the sales calendar for the retail industry. The January sales come in the wake of Christmas and more particularly the Boxing Day sales.

Retailers sell and conjure massive discounts as they bid to unload excess end of year stock before they restock and update lines for the New Year. So shoppers are wooed with discounts of up to 70%.

What happens during these sales is every business rule is broken. Instead of focusing on profit, retailers focus entirely on sales. I couldn't help but observe that there was total disregard for the security of the merchandises and storefronts ceased to function as instruments of marketing.

However, the first two points are not the topics of discussion in this chapter, therefore, I will limit my discussion to the third aspect which is the storefront.

A retail storefront serves three main purposes:

1) It is the image of the store and all that it represents
2) It serves as an effective marketing tool to attract customers into the store
3) It is the point of transition between the outside world and your store

Despite the significance of the storefront in retailing, too many retailers pay scant attention to this area. They spend most of their time getting the inside of their store design right and completely ignore the storefront.

For a start, the storefront window is the most expensive part of a retail space. It is considered to be equal to one third of the entire cost of the store rental. In his book: "Window and Interior Display – The Principles of Visual Merchandising", Robert Kretschmer reveals that *"A small store out of the high-rent district, with a rental of $100 a month, would put a yearly rental value of $400 on its window. Windows of the higher-class stores are often considered to be worth £20,000 a year or more. In New York City stores such as Macy's value their window space at more than $100,000 a year".*

Kretschmer feels that the value of the store window is based on the number of people who pass by it each day. "So" he explains *"in towns with populations ranging from 2500 to 25,000, window passers-by number between 372 per hour and 4,464 per day."*

To calculate the current value of your storefront, try *Kretschmer's* formula:

> *"The value of a window space is the basis upon which a charge against the merchandise department is determined. Two factors must be taken into consideration: (1) the comparative importance of the space and (2) the actual rental cost of the window. For example a store with 16 windows, 4 of them on a main thoroughfare and the remaining 12 on a side street carrying less traffic, would of course, place a higher rating on its 4 front windows.*
>
> *Windows one through four, on the main thoroughfare, would be rated highest in importance and value. Then, starting with window*

5 and down the side street to window 16; each window would diminish in value.

Assuming that each of the 4 front windows had an equal rental and budget cost of $18,200 a year, each department using one of them would be charged at that rate, or $60.66 a day (on the basis of 300 working days a year). Window number 16, with a rental and budget cost of only $4800 a year, would draw only $16.00 a day from the departments using it".

Based upon the above formula, calculate the value of your own storefront. You will grasp the importance of maximising its value.

In the beginning of the chapter, I outlined the result of my own research into storefront usage in the UK.

Figure 17: Even though the store front is the most valuable space in a retail store, most retailers do not make good use of the space

Figure 18: Successful retailers know the value of their storefront

When I took a trip around shopping centres in the UK, one observation I made which Kretschmer confirms in his book was that tier one retailers made proper use of their store windows. While tier two and independent retailers not knowing the value of their storefront, covered their entire storefront with discount signs.

> To quote Kretschmer again: *"the modern high-class store shows a few carefully chosen articles in a single unit of a display to create an atmosphere of quality and exclusivity of style. A store of this type may devote forty weeks a year to these simple, exclusive showings.*
>
> *Yet the same store can cram a window full of merchandise for its January white sale or its August housewares clearance or for its Christmas toy displays, without sacrificing any of its dignity.*
>
> *The character of the store is so firmly established by its regular display policy that these sporadic outbursts of high-powered sales promotions only accentuate the high-class rating of the store. The so called middle-class store has a tendency to crowd its display just a little.*
>
> *This store puts more merchandise in its windows than the high-class store, yet at the same time it strives to imitate the style of the quality store. Its aim then must be to attract some of the cream of the trade while still catering to the very profitable middle class."*

The lower-class store directs its attention mainly to the purchaser of low-priced goods. The windows of such a store are often crowded up to the hilt, more like the old-time general store. You can further identify this type of store by its inferior price tickets and gaudy show cards and banners.

Figures (1-5) show images of a tier one retailer. Figures (6-7) show images of tier two and three retailers during the January sales period. As you can see while tier one retailers only have a few sales signs in their windows, tier two and independent retailers cover their entire storefront with sale signs.

> *One of the most important elements of a storefront display is to tell the story of the display. Having a sign that says 70% as the only storefront display of a retail store tells customers that particular retailer has no story to tell.*

The general consensus in marketing is that people buy emotionally but justify their decisions rationally. To appeal to their emotions, you should have more than your price displayed at your storefront. Price is a single factor for which people buy and in most cases it's the least of the reasons why people buy.

Thirty up to 40% of customers will buy on price alone. However, up to 70% will buy on the basis of convenience, good customer experience and quality. Therefore, in order to persuade the large majority of people to enter your store, you need more than 70% discount stickers displayed at your storefront.

First and foremost you need to have a storefront display that triggers all of their buying emotions.

How to design an attractive storefront

The storefront needs to convey a clear message about your brand and products. The message must be simple, unambiguous and to the point that shoppers get it as they walk by. The decision to take a closer look at your display or enter your store depends on how attractive he (she) finds your storefront display.

There is a direct correlation between your storefront design and customer traffic. Traffic will increase if your storefront is designed to catch the eyes and get in to the psyche of shoppers as they pass by your store.

The power of your storefront is as much in its signage, as it is in its lighting; interactive window displays and visual merchandise displays.

Storefronts vary from one store to another. Depending on the type of retailer it can include wholesale stores, kiosks, barrows, market stalls and internet based retail stores. However, all retail storefronts must meet the following three objectives:

a) Attract shoppers attention
b) Entice shoppers to enter the store
c) Persuade them to buy

To meet the above objectives your storefront design must above all else, *represent your store image.*

Your storefronts should be an expression of your store's image. Your storefront has to be design in such a way that it expresses your store's individual identity.

Storefront entrance

Your door location and design are essential components of your storefront. They are the customer's transition from the outside world to your store. Your doors should place customers in the frame of mind of the type of experience they are about to receive. Consequently, it is advisable that doors provide direct link from the sidewalks or streets and should create a unique experience that distinguishes your store from other stores.

Storefront materials

Every component of your storefront needs to be purposefully designed to achieve your objective of attracting customer's attention. All materials used in the design need to be well thought through and of the highest quality. Your window needs to be designed in such a way that it creates a visual connection between the inside and outside of your store. Your entire storefront needs to be well glassed.

The most appropriate materials for a storefront are:

- Wood
- Metal
- Brick
- Stone
- Glass
- Concrete

Your storefront lighting system

A well-lit storefront is a must for the right store image. Effective lighting is good for merchandise displays as well as the safety of your customer and the general public. Sign lighting, including flat-mounted signs, blade and banner signs ought to be lit with covered or down lighting.

Lighting fixtures need to be positioned in such a way that they focus on the products on display not the window or street. When lighting fixtures are not positioned well, they either distract from the display or allow shadows that interfere with the display.

Your awnings

If your store has awnings ensure it is periodically cleaned to maintain the veracity of fabrics; seam and colour. Periodic cleaner also avoids the unnecessary expense of replacement. The awnings can be used as an effective marketing and image building tool. By placing information about your store on it you add feel to the streets cape and variety to the building façade.

It also saves the storefront displays from sun. Design and position should balance the scale of the store facade design.

The best types of awnings are retractable or open side as opposed to vinyl or internally lit awnings.

Signage

Your storefront signage illuminates the outside of your store and attracts customers like moths to a flame. Here the lighting also builds a sense of branding and brand engagement. The signage peeps into the souls of customers and creates a connection between them and your storefront signage.

This helps in the creation of brand awareness and brand loyalty. Your storefront signage needs to be incorporated into your entire storefront design and the store design itself.

Strategies for designing an attractive store

Display your finest products in your storefront window

Display your best and newest collection of products in your storefront window. However, avoid the temptation of cluttering the display with too many items. This would only confuse your customers. Displaying a few items with adequate space around them will allow each product to stand out. Ensure that the theme of the season is clearly visible in the display. Changing the theme of your displays on a constant basis will bring an aura of newness to the display.

Maintain a clean storefront

Your storefront ought to be clean and tidy at all times. You need to ensure that glass windows are sparkling clean to increase visibility; bricks and mortar buildings are pressure washed, wooden buildings are treated with vanish with a gloss finish and litter, leaves or any types of dirt is constantly removed from your store entrance.

Encourage curiosity with sidewalk sales

Extending your display to outside of your store, for example in the centre of the shopping centre, stirs curiosity. For loss prevention reasons, ensure the products displayed outside of your store are in inexpensive. Where ever possible display dummies. Remember the goal is to stimulate curiosity not to facilitate theft.

Make promotion and discount visible

This might seem to run contrary to what I said in an earlier chapter about displaying huge sales signs on your storefront. I am not suggesting that you display large signs that prevent shoppers from seeing your displays. There needs to be a balance between advertising and display. You need to ensure that customers are able to see the products on display while at the same time in a distinct yet visible manner make them aware of promotions and special offers.

Decorate storefront with plants

If possible enhance your storefront with plants. Placing plants at the entrance of your store sends very warm message of welcome to your customer and make them feel at home in your store.

There is almost a mystical or magical connection between humans and plants. Plants stimulate our natural senses especially in towns and cities, people want to have the opportunity to get closer to nature. Therefore, just having plants at the entrance of your store is enough to attract customers to your store.

Steps for designing an attractive store

Step One
Ensure your storefront is made entirely of glass with focal points, wooden cubes and shelves for merchandise.

Step Two
Fit awnings to protect shoppers viewing your displays, from rain, sun or snow.

Step Three
Install attractive and informative signage that is visible from the other side of the road and is easy to read. Signs should be hung on the outside of the building, front door and windows.

Step Four
Decorate the pavement of the door front with attractive tiles and ensure that door frames are big enough for all sizes of customers.

Step Five
Install an adequate lighting system at your storefront. Ensure proper lighting on display and the entrance as a whole.

Step Six
Paint your storefront with a vibrant colour; hang seasonal banners; flags or holiday decoration. Just do anything that would make your storefront standout.

Remember your storefront is the best and most inexpensive marketing tool at your disposal. Make full use of it and make sure that every decision you make about your storefront design is based on sound marketing principles.

Chapter Eight

How To Choose The Right Materials For Store Design

Design of a building starts with the concept or reason the building is to be designed. The next step is the development of the blueprint followed by the purchasing of the materials to construct the building.

Each of these aspects of a building is equally important because without the concept, the blueprint would not be created and without the materials the building would not be built.

In the last few chapters, we have dealt with the concept and the blueprint. This chapter is about showing you the best materials to use in the creation of a magnificent store design and why they are the best.

Retailing like any other business is very competitive. To compete in a crowded field, victory is possible once you have the ability to stand out from the crowd. Like most things in life, the difference between success and failure depends on doing the little things better than the rest of the field. In retailing one of those little things is to ensure that you acquire the right materials for your store design.

The three areas of your store design you really need to focus on are:

- Ceiling
- Walls
- Floor

In the rest of this chapter, I will introduce the most commonly used ceilings, walls and floors in retail store design and explain the benefits of using them.

Ceiling

I am quite aware that not a lot of people entering retail store raise their head to see how the ceiling looks. I promise you, there are a lot of people who will notice if your ceiling is not impressive. It is curious how thing like this works. When things are right, it is taken for granted. However, when things go wrong everyone notice them.

I introduce the concept because as I dive into the most commonly used types of ceilings, there is the tendency for many retailers especially tier two and three retailers to belief that people would not notice their ceiling.

> **When your ceiling looks good, hardly anyone will pay attention to it. That is a fact. However, if it is not presentable everyone will notice it, remember that.**

Ceilings are classified in accordance with their appearance or construction:

- Cathedral ceiling
- Cathedral ceiling is a tall ceiling area similar to that used in churches
- Dropped ceiling

Dropped ceilings are specifically used for aesthetic or practical purposes either to achieve a certain ceiling height or to provide space for piping.

Listed below are suggestions on what to consider as a good ceiling design:

Flat white ceiling

Figure 19: Flat white ceiling give the illusion of height

A flat white ceiling is necessary in a retail store with low ceiling. It gives the perception of height in a store with low ceiling.

Tin ceiling

Figure 20: Tin ceiling gives the store an elegant appearance

Tin ceilings can give your store an elegance appearance and draw customers' attention as they shop. The name tin ceilings originated from the material used for the ceiling during the Victorian era.

They are now available in different metallic finishes. Aluminium is the most commonly used type because unlike some other metals, aluminium does not corrode and is very light, flexible and reasonably priced.

Wooded ceiling

Figure 21: Wooded ceiling adds warmth and charm to the store

Using wooden panelling would add warmth and charm to your store and provide a subtle finish. Matching a wooden surface with other wooden surfaces such as wooden curtain poles or ornaments can result in a cohesive and stylish finish.

Acoustic Ceiling

Figure 22: Acoustic Ceiling are sound-absorbing ceiling

Acoustic ceiling tiles are sound-absorbing ceiling tiles dropped into grid metal strips suspended from the actual original ceiling of the store. They were originally developed by interior designers as a way of lowering ceilings and reducing the level of noise in a room.

In addition to reducing noise, acoustic ceilings can also conceal unattractive fixtures, wires and pipes that may be running along the ceiling of older buildings.

The following are the pros and cons of using acoustic ceilings:

Pros:

- Acoustic ceiling reduces sound between floors of building and inside the store making it comfortable for customers to carry on their shopping.
- Acoustic ceiling tiles are simple to maintain or replace and can be painted.

Cons:

- Panels can be easily damaged by moisture causing the panel to drop from the ceiling unexpectedly in extreme cases.

- Moisture damage show and dries leaving an unpleasant stain on the ceiling.

Gypsum board ceilings

Figure 23 & 24: Gypsum board ceilings are commonly used products

Gypsum board is a common product currently used for walls and ceilings in homes and stores. It is easy to install however, the installation of suspension system requires a professional installer.

Gypsum can be found in sedimentary rocks all around the world. A layer of gypsum sandwiched between two sheets of thick paper is known as Dry wall.

The pros and cons of gypsum board ceilings:

Pros:

- Gypsum board ceilings are relatively simple to install and are reasonably priced
- Gypsum ceiling tile provides variety of designs, acoustical and aesthetic qualities.

Cons:

- Gypsum board ceilings do not absorb sound very well.
- Gypsum board ceilings can be easily damaged. It is recommended you use chemically treated gypsum wallboard that is moisture resistant in a store that has high moisturised contents.

Plastic Ceiling

Figure 25: Plastic Ceiling are alternative to wood and tile

Plastic ceiling tiles are an alternative to wood or plaster tiles that are commonly used by a majority of retailers. Plastic ceilings are reasonably priced, strong and long lasting. They are very light in comparison to wood making it easier to work with them. They do not appear as elegant or presentable as acoustic tiles or gypsum board ceilings.

Aluminium Ceiling

Figure 26: Aluminium Ceiling will not rut or crack

Aluminium ceilings are very durable ceiling that would not rust or crack because they are made from a non-porous material. They are easy to install because they consist of different panels. They can be installed like acoustic ceiling and fitted to the main ceiling.

Walls

The decision of wall covering in your store should be based upon: style, ambience, theme, image and the practicality of maintenance. If you choose to paint your store, it is advisable to use washable paints.

The most commonly used materials for walls in a retail store are gypsum board (dry wall). Their surface has slots which allow pipes, cables and conduits to run through them. Retail walls are either full height or partial height.

Plaster walls can also be used in place of gypsum board. They can be moulded into different shapes enabling them to form curve or soffit walls which cannot be done with gypsum board walls. Plaster walls are more durable than gypsum board walls and can be used in other areas of the shopping centre.

Wall Covering

The most commonly used wall covering in retail space is painting. In addition to heavy-textured paints, the three main types of wall finishing are gloss, semi-gloss and flat.

Flat paints are suitable for walls, while gloss and semi-gloss are suitable for doors, trims and high contact areas.

Wall paper is another type of covering used in some retail stores. Wall papers need to be located in less contact areas; probably close to the ceilings.

Wood

Figure 27: A combination of soft and hard wooden walls are commonly used

Oak, red or white wood are the most common types of wooden wall finishing in retail stores. Combinations of hard and soft woods are constantly used depending on the preference of the retailer. Hard wood include walnut, rosewood, mahogany, ash, oak and teak, while softwoods are pine, birch, cedar and redwood.

Hardboard, metal and plastic wall panelling

Figure 28: Hardboard panelling is an inexpensive thin particle board

Hardboard panelling is an inexpensive thin particle board about a quarter inch thick, composing materials that simulate solid wood. They can also be found in laminated tambour created to achieve batter effect.

Panelling or laminated plastic made from three quarter inch particle board layers of plastics which can be custom designed for individual retail stores. Plastic laminates are very durable and available in different colours, finishes and patterns and easy to clean but susceptible to chipping at the corners.

Metal laminates are also very durable especially when laminated to particle board. They are available in different types and finishes, stainless steel, aluminium, copper and brass.

Glass Walls

Figure 29: Glass is not easy to work with

Mirrors are used to create the illusion of extra space or reflect images. Mirrors are available in clear, grey and bronze finishes and are about a quarter thick. Glass is not particularly easy to work with, therefore the design needs to be uncomplicated.

Tile Walls

Figure 30: Tile Walls is durable and offers great degree of flexibility

Ceramic tiles can also be used as a wall finishing and are available in different sizes, shapes and colours. Terrazo is also very durable wall finishing that offers great degree of flexibility.

Flooring

Flooring is another very important component of retail store design. Unlike the ceiling, customers actually look at the flooring when they enter the store, therefore, it is imperative that you lay good flooring in your store.

Carpeting is the most widely used flooring type in the retail industry for the obvious reason that it is reasonably priced and comes in a variety of colours and textures and it has significant sound absorbing properties.

Other flooring materials used are:

- Resilient floors
- Wooded floors
- Non-resilient floors

Ceramic tile flooring

Figure 31: Ceramic tile is a very durable surface used for any type of application

Ceramic tile is a very durable surface that is recommended for basically any type of application. Ceramic is water resistant and there are porcelain tiles which are frost resistant and frost proof in some cases.

Ceramic tiles are so far the favourite retail flooring because they are highly resistant to moisture, stain and wear. They are generally produced in larger sizes and are suitable for large retail areas.

Vinyl composition flooring

Figure 32: Vinyl composition tiles are also widely used because they are very durable

Vinyl composition tiles are also widely used because they are very durable and the tiles bump flush together.

There are two types of vinyl floors:

Printed vinyl containing fillers of durability are made by imprinting a design on a film over a vinyl base.

Solid vinyl is widely preferred in high-traffic retail stores as the colour and pattern go through the entire thickness.

Eco tile flooring

Figure 33: Eco tile is an attractive and hardwearing interlocking floor tile

Eco tile is an attractive and hardwearing interlocking floor tile. It is designed to allow quick and simple glue less installation. They are thick and durable and are popular amongst retailers. Eco tile floor finishes are also low maintenance and last significantly longer than conventional vinyl or any other carpet alternative.

Listed below are tips for choosing your store materials:

- Select materials that are modern
- Select materials that are extremely durable
- Select materials that are quick and easy to install

- Select materials with good anti-slip properties
- Select materials that are easy to clean and maintain
- Select materials that are dynamic can be easily changed if the situation demands
- Select materials that are ideal for oily substrates

Chapter Nine

How To Design A Profitably Retail Store

In chapter two, I outlined the three factors responsible for Harrods phenomenal success as:

- Good store design
- Attractive visual merchandise display
- Effective loss prevention strategy

The subject of loss prevention is something that has never been taken seriously by the retail industry even though the industry spends billions each year on loss prevention. In fact in the last ten years, loss prevention spending has increased tremendously. In 2011 retail spending on loss prevention rose to $128 billion, however, in the same period retail shrinkage rose to $119 billion.

So why is it that despite the huge amount spent on loss prevention, retail shrinkage continues to rise?

To answer this question, let's take a peek into Harrods loss prevention strategy.

Harrods store design and visual merchandising displays are definitely factors in its success. However, the key factor responsible for Harrods' success is its ability to remain profitable. And in business, profit is king.

In retail the formula for making profit is to increase sales and reduce shrinkage.

Increasing sales requires good store design and attractive visual merchandising. Reducing shrinkage requires an effective loss prevention strategy.

So what do Harrods and most successful retailers have over the rest in the retail industry? It is their ability to simultaneously increase sales and reduce shrinkage. Most retailers know how to increase sales, but when it comes to reducing their shrinkage, they are challenged.

Getting these two right is the fundamental principle of retail success. No retailer can succeed without simultaneously increasing sales and reducing shrinkage.

Why does shrinkage reduction or loss prevention measures fail in most retail organisations?

Loss prevention measures fail as a result of the following:

- Lack of understanding of the subject
- Senior management's failure to prioritise
- Outsourcing loss prevention without a mechanism for accountability
- Inexperienced loss prevention managers
- Ineffective use of loss prevention technology

Harrods is the first retail store that I have ever entered that has no visible blind spots. I am not suggesting that there are absolutely no blind spots as I managed to spot a few.

However, the difference with other stores is that Harrods' blind spots are invisible to the untrained eyes.

Anyone deciding to shoplift in Harrods would have to be:

- A professional shoplifter or part of an organised retail crime syndicate
- Really brave
- Really stupid

Products are displayed in such a manner that each department seems wide open. Store employees standing at one end of a department have a clear view of the entire department.

There is CCTV in every corner of the store. In addition to electronic surveillance store assistants buzz around like bees and make it difficult for anyone who might be intending on shoplift.

I am not saying that it is impossible to shoplift from Harrods. Far from that, shoplifting prevention requires the implementation of a combination of strategies. However, by adopting their type of store design, displaying their products in the manner that they are displayed and taking other loss prevention measures, Harrods has drastically reduced the possibility of shoplifting.

Now contrast Harrods loss prevention strategy with a top ten UK retailer that I once worked for as a store detective.

A few years back, I was employed as a store detective for a leading retailer in the UK. On my very first day at work, whilst in the middle of briefing with the officer I was relieving, I noticed a couple walk into the store and head towards the coat section.

I stood there perplexed as I witnessed the lady remove one of the coats from the hanger, try it on, and then casually walk to the exit with her partner and scurry into the waiting getaway car. £900 walked out the door with such incredible ease, made me think "Holy cow! How can this sort of thing happen in broad daylight?"

The answer was actually quite apparent: The coats were prominently displayed right close to the exit.

Keeping this experience as a vivid reminder, any time I was assigned to a different store, I took great care to walk around and look for high ticket items that were not securely displayed. I would call the store manager over and advise that the items be relocated to more secure locations within the store. To my disbelief, most managers failed to take my advice – in their eyes, I am merely a store detective. What did I know about proper merchandising?

As a second example: I was working at a store in London Colney, immediately upon entering the store I noticed coats worth £250 prominently displayed near the store entrance. I located the store manager and expressed my concern to him.

I even joked with him how even the CIA Director at the time, George Tenant, could not possibly protect those coats where they were positioned. This manager ignored my warning. A few hours later, some of the coats were stolen, just as I had predicted.

When I approached the manager again, I figured he would pay more attention to me now that my gloomy prediction had come true. Once again, he failed to heed my warning only paying attention to me after 20 out of the 25 coats had been stolen.

At this same location, there are two big retailers who shared a single toilet facility located outside of both stores. Shoplifters knew this and would steal from one store, head to the direction of the toilet, pass through the other store and escape. When they were stopped and questioned by our store security, they would mention they were on their way to the toilet.

They were technically correct about the direction they were heading given the location of the toilet. The location of the toilet caused both stores to lose thousands pounds to shoplifting. Yet neither store's management could pin-point the location of the toilet as one of the primary causes of their shrinkage.

I share these stories with you to emphasize a very important point: Shoplifting occurs in most retail stores simply because it is allowed to take place.

> *Shoplifting is a crime of opportunity, eliminate the opportunity and you reduce its possibility.*

To increase sales yet fail to reduce profit draining activities is false economy. Many retailers feel loss prevention is something that they could do if they had the resources. The reality is: it is something that you cannot afford not to do because no retailer can become profitable without implementing effective loss prevention measures.

Inexperienced loss prevention managers

Ninety to 95% of retail loss prevention department managers are ex-service personnel. As a result of their law enforcement background, they take the law enforcement approach to their work. They focus mainly on arresting shoplifters and dishonest employees.

While it is true that shoplifting and employee theft accounts for almost 70% of retail shrinkage, they are not the sole cause of shrinkage. Furthermore, shoplifting and employee dishonesty cannot be tackled by solely arresting individuals. Preventative measures such as good store design and visual merchandise displays, as I mentioned in the case of Harrods, are the key to shrinkage reduction.

However, due to the fact that the majority of retail loss prevention managers know very little about store design and visual merchandising, they are unable to incorporate these aspects into their loss prevention strategies. As a result most loss prevention measures fail.

> *"The average retailer makes a 1% net profit out of each dollar and the average industry shrinkage percentage is 2.6%. This means that shrinkage is almost three times the average retailer's profit margin. By reducing retail shrinkage to 50% – from 2.6 cents to 1.3 cents, a retailer could more than double his profits: from 1 cent to 2.3 cents".*
> (Crosset Company newsletter, June 2010)

Outsource Loss Prevention

Some retailers outsource their loss prevention department to outside contractors. As laudable as this may seem, it is a seriously flawed idea because retailers are sometimes incapable of clearly articulating their expected outcome.

When a job is outsourced, there is usually an expected outcome. However, if the retailer outsourcing the job cannot articulate their expected outcome, it is difficult to hold the contractor accountable.

Wal-Mart founder Sam Walton once described retail shrinkage as a "profit killer". He was right. High shrinkage is responsible for the death of many retail organisations.

The benefit of a good store design is to increase sales with the use of attractive merchandising display. However, attractive display does not necessarily mean designing your store without developing mechanism for crime prevention.

As you develop your store design blueprint, you need to ensure that the safety of the products is paramount. In the final analysis you are in business to make profit. You cannot make profit if you increase sales at the expense of the security of your products.

Without losing the original purpose of your store design, you can apply changes to the way fixtures are arranged in your store in order to decrease the chances of theft.

> *One way of doing this is to locate smaller items in places that are visible to employees. Furthermore, positioning employees in key areas of the store is a good shoplifting prevention strategy.*

Larger products need to be placed in small quantities to prevent the store from appearing cluttered. Poor display of large products can obscure the view of employees and increase the possibility for shoplifting.

Aisles and shelves need to be properly labelled to ensure customers can easily and quickly locate products.

In addition to labelling, installing proper lighting will attract buyers to products as well as allow your employees to observe the surroundings more effectively.

There is no fail proof way of preventing shoplifting. However, the installation of security systems such as CCTV and mirrors can reduce incidence of shoplifting in your store. Security mirrors optimize employee's view of the store and reduce blind spots.

How to increase your sales and simultaneously increase your profit?

The following are effective steps for increasing sales and profit with a good store design:

Step 1:
Locate smaller products close to areas that employees frequently visit to reduce the risk of shoplifting.

Step 2:
Reduce the number of large products on display to allow store employees unhindered views of the store.

Step 3:

Position employees in key locations of the store to increase overall security.

Step 4:

Security mirrors in the store to reduce blind spots and increase surveillance.

Step 5:

Use CCTV in areas that are not regularly frequented by employees and place high ticket products under cameras.

Step 6:

Ensure your loss prevention department is involved in the planning of your store design blueprint.

Years ago, shoplifting was conducted by homeless and drug addicts wanting to feed their habit. Today shoplifting is conducted by retail crime gangs using more sophisticated methods, never before seen in the industry. Within four minutes, an organised retail crime gang could steal seven thousand pounds worth of products from your store.

Think about this when developing your store design blueprint.

Chapter Ten

The Best Store Design Technologies

Technology can enhance the process of your store design and enable you to achieve your objectives of increasing sales and profit. However, in order to derive the maximum benefit from any technology; it is essential that you choose the most appropriate technology for your store and target market.

There is no one size fit all when it comes to the acquisition and implementation of technology. Consequently, prior to the acquisition of store design technology, it is imperative that you give consideration to the desired outcome of the technology.

Here are seven questions you should answer prior to investing in store design technology:

1) What are the types of store design technologies available?
2) What are their functionalities including features and benefits?
3) What constraints do they diminish?
4) Where can they be sourced?
5) What policies and procedures helped you to operate without those technologies?
6) What policies and procedures should you put in place now to adapt to the new technologies?
7) Are the technologies future-proof?

Answering the above questions would guide you in your decision of selecting the most appreciated store design technologies for your store.

The use of technology is essential for any retail operation. Whatever the size of the retail store, technology has both tangible and intangible benefits and helps to increase profit, increase productivity and improve customer satisfaction.

In order to provide convenience and a unique shopping experience for your customers, listed below are examples of the latest retail technologies in the market:

Information kiosk:

- Provides information on locating products in a store
- Is valuable for displaying promotional and advertising information
- It can be used in a shopping centre to show location of stores

Satellite navigation software:

- Helps shoppers find products by using an app that runs on Smart phones
- Speeds up shopping by showing customers a 3-D store map and the shortest route to pick up everything they need

Sensormatic Safer Electronic Article Surveillance (EAS) Solutions:

- With Sensormatic Safer Electronic Article Surveillance customers now have the freedom to openly select high value items without waiting for store associates. Specific area of the store could be fitted with the system.
- High ticket items have safe lock to prevent shoplifting

Radio Frequency Identification (RFID technology):

- Provides retailers with an advanced bar coding system as no line-of-sight is required to read a product with an RFID tag

- Automates the retail supply chain, reducing labour costs, human error and time spent checking in products
- Is less susceptible to damage as it is placed on a product or embedded in plastic to withstand harsh environmental conditions such as moisture, exposure to chemicals and outdoors

Point-Of-Sale system (POS Technology)

- Records sales as they occur and provides detailed inventory report
- Solves a variety of operational and record-keeping problems
- Can be customised to meet your specific requirements
- Can quickly locate sale prices and costs of all products
- Help determine the causes of shrinkage
- Records marked downs and discounts
- Tracks promotion successfully and easily
- Accurately reveals the effect of promotions
- Helps monitor store associate activity and productivity
- Ensures product prices are consistent in multiple retail operations
- Can be integrated into other software providers packages such as expenses, payroll or staff attendance software
- Helps in effective workflow distribution to accurately monitor activity of each store associate
- Provides accurate customer profile: buying behaviour, addresses or emails
- Facilitates an easy payment method

A lot of new retail technologies are constantly introduced into the market. I have chosen to focus on the main ones that can be integrated into other types of technologies. Most importantly, they can all be used for loss prevention purposes. It is a fact of life that new technologies are obsolete within three years of invention.

This means that you need to always be on the look-out for new technologies that would increase your productive capacity, staff productivity and ultimately your profit margin.

Summary

Since 2007, twenty-four thousand four hundred and forty-six (24,446) large and medium size retail stores close down resulting in two hundred and nineteen thousand five hundred and two thousand (219,502) retail staff losing their jobs.

These days, one can almost walk around the High Street and take a bet with hundred per cent accuracy on which High Street retailer will be out of business the next week, month or year.

If someone was to place a gun to my head and force me to choose the top five High Street retailers who will cease to exist five years from today, my pick will be the following:

- PC World
- Staples
- WH Smith
- HMV
- Dixons

When they eventually close shop, they will blame the recession and difficult trading conditions.

However, what I have proved in this books is, success or failure in retail has little to do with external factors.

Retailers fail because they do not give thought to the things we have discussed in this book. It is my hope that you immediately put the information you have learnt into action in your business.

I have tried to make the information as practical as possible in order for them to be easily implemented. I have done my part, it is your turn.

Good luck!

Great Books by Romeo

Book Romeo now!
+44(0)78 650 49508
romeo@theprofitexperts.co.uk

27.9% The Most Effective Retail Shrinkage Reduction Technologies

Prior to investing in any technology, there are vital questions that need to answered; those questions along with their answers can be found in this e-book.

This e-book was conceived out of our own desperate efforts to answer those questions.

What you will learn:

- Technologies That Prevent Employee Theft
- Technologies That Prevent Shoplifting

- Receiving Technologies
- Multi-purpose Technologies

12.24% The Most Effective Retail Employee Error Reduction Strategies

Employee errors in pricing, accounting and receiving contribute approximately 18% of retail shrinkage; this equates to £18,623 in losses to an average supermarket or store and almost £49,679 in losses to a superstore. This means that a store or supermarket that operates with a 1% net profit will need to make an additional £3million in annual sales in order to recover profit lost due to employee errors. By the same measure a typical hyper store will need to increase its sales by £8million.

You will learn:

- Constitutes as Retail Employee Error
- to Calculate the Cost of Employee Error
- to Calculate Additional Sales Required to Recover Losses Caused by Employee Error
- of Employee Error
- to Reduce Employee Error
- Ultimate Employee Error Prevention Formula
- to Apply the Lessons from This E-Book to Your Business

43.5% The Most Effective Retail Profit Protection Strategies

The retail landscape is changing rapidly with the constant increase in internet shopping. From 2005 to 2009, the online shopping population grew to 1.6 billion.

It is predicted to rise to 2.3 billion by 2014 with gross revenue totalling $778.6 billion. This is bad news for traditional brick and mortar retail businesses.

The question is: are you prepared? You will find your answer in this eBook.

What you will learn:

- The Conventional Approach to Loss prevention
- Why Loss Prevention is Critical to Retail
- Loss Prevention Spending vs Return on Investment
- What You Are Losing
- Profit vs Sales Calculation
- How to Create a Culture of Loss Prevention
- Effective Shrinkage Management Strategies
- The Ultimate Profit Protection Formula

24.5% The Most Effective Perishable And Non-Perishable Shrinkage Reduction Strategies

This e-book is jam packed with information on the causes of retail shrinkage, types of retail shrinkage, the cost of shrinkage to the retail industry and how shrinkage can be prevented. It is a comprehensive e-book on how and why shrinkage occurs and it provides a step-by-step guide on how to prevent shrinkage.

You will learn:

- An Introduction to Perishable Shrinkage
- Breakdown of Perishable Shrinkage
- Causes of Perishable Shrinkage
- How to Prevent Perishable Shrinkage
- The Ultimate Perishable Shrinkage Prevention Formula
- An Introduction to Non-Perishable Shrinkage
- Classification of Non-Perishable Shrinkage
- Breakdown of Non-Perishable Shrinkage

- Strategies for Preventing Non-Perishable Shrinkage
- The Ultimate Non-Perishable Shrinkage Prevention Formula
- How to Apply The Lessons From This E-Book to Your Business

27.8% The Most Effective Retail Employee Theft Reduction Strategies

The majority of retail employees are decent people who go to work each day to serve their customers and make their living.

However, there are the rotten apples that contaminate the good names of the rest.

This e-book is an instructional guide to retailers to show them how to minimise and prevent employee theft in their stores. Like shoplifting most incidents of employee theft occur because the opportunity exists. When retailers remove the opportunity, they can reduce the possibilities. This e-book will show retailers how to remove the opportunities that allow employee theft in their stores.

You will learn:

- Why Employees Steal
- The Process of Employee Theft
- Signs of Employee Theft
- How to Calculate the Cost of Employee Theft
- How to Prevent Employee Theft
- How Technology Can Help Prevent Employee Theft
- The Ultimate Employee Theft Prevention Formula

84%: The Most Effective Strategies for Increasing Retail Profit

The formula for increasing profit in retail is to increase sales and reduce shrinkage. How can retailers increase sales and reduce shrinkage? The answer is in this book.

You will learn everything you need to know about:

- Creating a Culture of Loss Prevention
- Employee Error
- Employee Theft
- Shoplifting
- Perishable and Non-Perishable Shrinkage
- Receiving Shrinkage
- Technologies that Help to Reduce Retail Shrinkage

Visual Merchandise: How to Create a Beautiful Yet Profitable Display

Merchandise display is the most effective form of advertising for a retail store. The more attractive a display, the higher the possibility of increasing sales. This book will show retailers how to create a display that is so attractive that it would increase their footfall tenfold.

You will learn:

- The psychology behind visual merchandising
- How to use visual merchandising to increase retail sales
- Challenges facing visual merchandisers
- How to burst the price myth with creative merchandise display
- The best merchandise display strategies
- How to maximise display space allocation with creative fixtures
- The pros and cons of using a planogram
- The pros and cons of hiring visual merchandising companies
- Most effective visual merchandise technologies
- How to display merchandise for maximum profit

Store Design Blueprint: How to Design an Attractive But Profitable Store

There are three fundamental principles that underpin a retail store design:

1. Attract customers as they pass by the store
2. Entice them to enter the store
3. Persuade them to buy

The aim of this book is to show retailers how to apply these principles to this store design.

You will learn:

- Store design psychology – what you must know to succeed

- Store design – Image selling
- How to use store design to increase sales
- Store design for increased customer flow
- Choosing your store colour and layout
- The best retail store lighting system
- How to wow customers with creative storefront design
- How to choose the right materials for store design
- Designing store for profit – design security
- Store design technologies

How to Market and Manage A Professional Firm Series: How to make 7 Figure annually as a doctor, dentist, accountant, lawyer, consultant and private security firm owner.

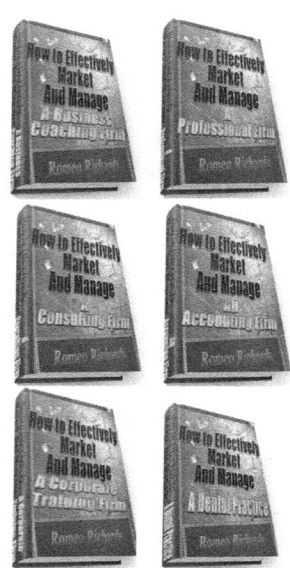

There are four elements essential for the success of any business:

1. Visionary leadership
2. Great people

3. Good system

4. Good marketing system

In the How to Market and Manage A Professional Firm Series, we teach professional entrepreneurs how to effectively utilize these four elements for the development of their businesses.

Many professionals are good technicians. They are good at their professions, however, when it comes to running business they are challenged.

The aim of the 7 Figure Code Books Series is to show professionals how to enhance their technical skills and apply similar levels of structural thinking into building a 7 Figure business.

There is no reason why a doctor or lawyer should not be able to easily make 7 Figure per annum. We show them how to achieve this in the How to Market and Manage A Professional Firm Series.

You will learn:

- How to create an effective business system that runs on auto-pilot
- How to recruit and retain only top talents
- How to develop an effective marketing system
- How to create new market for a product or service
- How the attract new clients and retain existing ones

Book Romeo

Book Romeo now by calling:
+44(0)78 650 49508
Or email: romeo@theprofitexperts.co.uk

www.ingramcontent.com/pod-product-compliance
Lightning Source LLC
Chambersburg PA
CBHW051709170526
45167CB00002B/591